ULTIMATE RETREAT EFFECT

Harnessing the Power
of Innovation Through Pause

NATASA DENMAN

First published by Ultimate World Publishing 2025
Copyright © 2025 Natasa Denman

ISBN
Paperback - 978-1-923425-67-5
Ebook - 978-1-923425-68-2

Natasa Denman has asserted her rights under the Copyright, Designs and Patents Act 1988 to be identified as the author of this work. The information in this book is based on the author's experiences and opinions. The publisher specifically disclaims responsibility for any adverse consequences which may result from use of the information contained herein. Permission to use information has been sought by the author. Any breaches will be rectified in further editions of the book.

All rights reserved. No part of this publication may be reproduced, stored in or introduced into a retrieval system, or transmitted in any form, or by any means (electronic, mechanical, photocopying, recording or otherwise) without the prior written permission of the author. Any person who does any unauthorised act in relation to this publication may be liable to criminal prosecution and civil claims for damages. Enquiries should be made through the publisher.

Cover design: Ultimate World Publishing
Layout and typesetting: Ultimate World Publishing
Editor: Alex Floyd-Douglass

Ultimate World Publishing
Diamond Creek,
Victoria Australia 3089
www.writeabook.com.au

DEDICATION

To anyone who deserves to take a break,
before burnout or ill health forces you to.

Take a pause.

Take a breath.

Sometimes the most productive thing you can do is…rest.

CONTENTS

Dedication	iii
Introduction: Ultimate Retreat Effect	1
Chapter 1 - Natasa Denman: The Formula	5
Chapter 2 - Vivienne Mason: Just Imagine	17
Chapter 3 - Julie Fisher: Opportunities	31
Chapter 4 - Wendy Trevarthen: Finding Courage Beyond the Waves	45
Chapter 5 - Carmen Hill: How One Woman's 'Yes' Became a Life-Changing Legacy	57
Chapter 6 - Felicity Lucke: Gaining Freedom and Healing	77
Chapter 7 - Claire White: From Burnout to Crystal-Claire Brilliance	89
Chapter 8 - Christine Judd: The Power of Showing Up	101
Chapter 9 - Sydney Francis: Beyond Metamorphosis	115

Chapter 10 - Alicia Buxton: Learn and Gain from
    Like-Minded People   127

Chapter 11 - Zoe MacBean: Just Start,
    Then Keep Moving. Your Path Will Appear   137

Chapter 12 - Lisa Dwyer: Never, Never Give Up   149

Afterword   163

Acknowledgements   165

Appendix A: Nat's Packing Checklist for
    Tropical Destinations   173

Appendix B: Workbook   177

INTRODUCTION
ULTIMATE RETREAT EFFECT

Do you often wonder where your spark went? Those ideas that used to supercharge you to action seem to have disappeared into oblivion and you ponder to yourself: Is this all there is? You could be suffering from 'same-same' blindness. This is when every day seems like groundhog day and your life feels like it's on autopilot.

I've seen too often people go years and sometimes decades without taking a break from their everyday work and life. I grew up in Macedonia and an annual holiday was not a 'Should we?' but a 'We must.' Even if finances were tight, people always made a priority for at least the annual summer holiday with family and friends.

When I immigrated to Australia, I came across so many people that simply never took holidays. I found this really strange. But when do you get to rest and recharge? Apparently, people just didn't prioritise this. Now that I have lived in Australia for more than 30 years, I do see Aussies as a culture that enjoys having a lifestyle and my fellow American friends and clients admire the balanced lifestyle Aussies live, because apparently you only get one to two weeks off a year in the US for a break. I guess there are different ways people and cultures prioritise leisure time.

I started my business more than 15 years ago and I have to say I never want to relive my first three years. I didn't have the capacity to take a break, and I felt like I was on 24/7. I am not sure if you have heard this quote that rings so true:

> "Entrepreneurs live a few years of their life like more people won't, so they can live the rest of their lives like most people can't." (Unknown)

This quote has resonated so much with me and how my life as an entrepreneur has unfolded. I am so glad, I put in all that work and effort to create something that supports me, my family, team and clients. It wasn't easy but totally worth it. So, what does this have to do with the title of this book: *Ultimate Retreat Effect*.

Well, I have run over 50, high-end *Ultimate 48 Hour Author Retreats* and now two international *Bond and Beyond Retreats*, in and amongst having travelled four months of each year and working the other eight for the past 12 years. What I have noticed is the power of taking a break and setting time aside for rest, recharging and innovation. You may think, taking time off to chill may kill your momentum, but I find that it's quite the opposite.

In spontaneous times of travel, rest and relaxation is when our best innovative ideas are born. When we are at the office, working our regular hours, we call this 'focused time'. Not much creativity or innovation comes during focused work as we tick off our never-ending to-do lists.

INTRODUCTION

Currently, I am writing this introduction at Ho Chi Minh airport waiting to board a flight to Nha Trang for a 10-night holiday with my family during the Easter break in Australia. No one is vying for my attention, my phone is not connected, my internet is off, and my family are all doing their own thing on their devices as we wait to board our delayed flight. This book is being birthed in a time of spontaneity.

What you will be reading for the rest of the book hasn't even happened yet. I am writing it before the fact, as I am 100% certain at the upcoming *Bond and Beyond Retreat* in Bintan, magic will unfold. 20 of my authors and team are coming together to chill, bond, network and without even trying to give birth to innovative new ideas for their lives, books and businesses.

Doing less, actually enables us to achieve more. Stripping your life back to take only actions that align with your top five values is what will give you your dream lifestyle and business.

This book is here to unpack the experience of different people, taking a retreat without too much structure and provide inspiration and insight of how it added value to their life and business. What will they do once this break is over? Will life continue on as it is, or will there be a new trajectory that will level up their experience moving forward? Keep reading and find out.

Who is this Book For?

If you are a busy, burnout professional, employee or business owner that keeps feeling like you must keep doing more and more and keep adding to your to-do list, it's time to stop and take the few hours it will take you to read this book before you put anything more on your list. Maybe the only thing that needs to be added is you booking yourself into the next retreat.

How to Use this Book?

You have started in the right spot; I recommend reading the first chapter and then freely skipping between the different chapters written by the retreat participants and go to the ones that you feel most drawn to. There is no need to read these in order as they are individual to that each person. Just like a TV series that has a plot line for each episode and does not connect, so does every chapter you see in this book written by each of the authors.

Life is too short to work ourselves to the bone. Work hard but play harder. Work to live and bank those memories which are the thing that you ultimately retire on. People think that retirement is all about having money, whereas I am a big believer that it's about having a brain bank full our memories.

So, let's get started!
Love, Natasa

CHAPTER 1 - NATASA DENMAN

THE FORMULA

*"The quality of your life is determined
by how many holidays you take."*
(Mira Haralampieva)

Hey there! My chapter will be less about the experience in Bintan, but more about being the host of a life-changing retreat. When you are the host, you get to experience it differently, you have responsibilities that the others don't and switching off is unlikely. However, I have plenty of time for my own chillaxing holidays with family and myself.

This trip was to really **bond**, have fun and utilise the power of masterminding and community. I wanted to create a group of people that would take a break together, mixed in with some structure and a lot of spontaneity where magic would happen. So how I'd like to add value to you, the reader, is for you to have a proven repeatable formula, so that this can happen in your life regularly with people you love to hang out with.

There are seven steps to follow every single year.

Here is the overview:

1. Plan early and block out time in your calendar
2. Find a like-minded community and become a part of it
3. Be travel ready
4. Set and share your Intention
5. Be a Chatty Charlie
6. Reflect and stay in touch
7. Do it again and again and again

Let's dive into detail for the above seven steps:

1. Plan early and block out time in your calendar

Now, if you know me, you know I'm a big believer in locking in my year before it begins. Every September, I sit down and plan out the entire next year – yep, all 12 months. It's not just about work and business planning. I start by putting in school holidays, public holidays, and then I go hunting for the best early bird deals on retreats, accommodation, and flights. When you plan early, you save big – sometimes thousands.

But planning ahead isn't just about saving money. It's also about creating space. Space for rest. Space for joy. Space for connection. I factor in solo getaways at least once or twice a year where I can reflect, think deeply, and reconnect with myself. Then I plan my family time – whether that's one-on-one trips with each of my three kids, or getaways with the whole family. And of course, I schedule my retreat-style group trips – the ones where I connect with like-minded people in similar seasons of life, with shared passions and values.

Here's the golden rule: what gets scheduled, gets done. That's why when I do my yearly planning, the first things I lock in are the breaks, retreats, and holidays. All the work, meetings, and commitments go around that. Your time to recharge shouldn't be the leftover scraps – it should be the foundation you build everything else on.

So if you want to bring more connection, joy, and clarity into your life each year, start with the calendar. Prioritise the time away. Book early. Plan ahead. And make it non-negotiable.

2. Find a like-minded community and become a part of it

One of the most powerful ways to get the absolute best out of a retreat experience is to do it with people who are not only in the same stage of life as you, but also share your interests, values and energy. When you're surrounded by the right people, the connection, fun, and growth that happens is on a whole different level.

So start by asking yourself: are you already part of a group you love? Maybe it's your local gym community – I actually did two retreats with my gym crew and honestly, they were some of the most connected, rewarding experiences. We already saw each other regularly, so being away together just deepened those bonds even more.

For me, my authors' community has become the heart of this. It's how the *Bond and Beyond Retreat* came to life – an annual international adventure where we get to blend business, relaxation, and personal growth, all with people who just get it.

If you're lucky enough to already be in a group like that, start there. See if they already run group trips – or, if they don't, why not suggest it? You could even take the lead and host your own, or co-create one with others. A great idea is to rotate who takes the lead each year, so you share the planning and everyone gets to be fully present at least some of the time.

Now, if you're reading this and thinking, 'Well, I don't have a group like that...' Don't worry. There are so many options out there. Check out *Meetup*, *Facebook* groups, or local clubs in your area. You'd be surprised how many communities organise retreats or wellness trips. Join one, head along to something that sparks your interest, and just give it a go.

The main thing is – don't do life alone. Find your tribe. Grow with them. Travel with them. Make memories with people who lift you up and leave you feeling more like yourself than ever.

3. Be travel ready

Let's be real – nothing puts a damper on your retreat buzz like arriving at the airport only to find out you can't check in because your passport is too close to expiry. Yep, it happens. And it's the kind of stress you just don't want when you're about to head off for an amazing trip.

So here's rule number one: always, always make sure you've got at least six months left on your passport before you travel internationally. That's a non-negotiable.

Over the years, I've figured out a few systems that make travel so much smoother—and I want to share those with you so you can focus on enjoying the journey, not stressing about the details.

One of my best tips? Create reusable packing checklists. I have two that I use regularly – one for summer locations and one for winter – and they live in a folder on my computer. Before each trip, I just open it up, tweak it for that particular destination, and print it out. Too easy.

And because I love making life easier, I've included my tropical location packing checklist for you at the end of this chapter. It's helped me travel light while still feeling prepared and stylish—and I know it'll help you too.

Next, let's talk packing cubes. These are a total game-changer. They keep everything organised inside your suitcase and make unpacking (and repacking!) a breeze. And while we're at it – sort yourself out a second toiletries bag. If you travel often, don't waste time packing and unpacking the same stuff. Just buy doubles of your essentials and keep them permanently in your suitcase. That way, you're always ready to go.

If you're planning more than one international trip in a year, I also highly recommend investing in annual travel insurance. It's much better value than buying a new policy every time you travel—and it gives you peace of mind so you can fully relax.

And finally – your suitcase. Invest in a good quality, lightweight one. My go-to brand is *Samsonite*. It's durable, roomy, and super light, which means more room for shopping and souvenirs! For example, on our most recent trip, I was away for three weeks and only packed nine kilos on the way over in my large *Samsonite* case. I came back with 30 kilos – souvenirs, clothes, gifts – the lot! So, don't be fooled by the size of the checklist. It's mostly small, clever essentials that won't take up much space.

So, before you jet off, get yourself travel-ready. Do the prep, organise your gear, and set yourself up for an easy, stress-free escape.

4. Set and share your intention

One of the most powerful things you can do before you head off on any retreat or trip – especially one with a group – is to get really clear on why you're going. What do you want to walk away with? Is it inspiration? A few new business ideas? A deeper connection with yourself or others? Or maybe you just need to unwind and shake off the noise of everyday life.

Whatever it is, decide on it before you go.

I always recommend taking a few quiet minutes to write out your intention by hand before a retreat. Not typed – handwritten. There's something magical about putting pen to paper. It grounds your thoughts and gives your intention power.

Once you arrive, share your intention with someone. It might be the retreat host or facilitator – someone who can guide or support you in making it happen. You might even find yourself drawn to someone in the group who becomes your buddy for the trip. Why not have a little group chat and swap intentions? It's a beautiful way to connect with others right from the start.

But here's the other side of the coin – don't overthink it or put pressure on yourself. Retreats are a space for calm, clarity, and spontaneity. Sometimes the best breakthroughs happen when you're not chasing them. So set the intention, absolutely – but then let go and allow the magic of the moment to unfold naturally.

You never know what conversations, connections, or lightbulb moments are just waiting for you when you create space to simply be.

5. Be a 'Chatty Charlie'

When you head off on a retreat or a trip with others, one of the best things you can do is lean into conversation. Even if you're not naturally outgoing, I encourage you to make the effort to talk, connect, and listen – because more often than not, your best ideas will come from conversations with others.

This is what we call the power of the mastermind. It's not just about your own thoughts – it's about what happens when your ideas spark off someone else's. That beautiful back-and-forth can be absolute gold. So even if you're an introvert, find those one-on-one moments where you can connect. It might be over breakfast, during a walk, or while you're relaxing by the pool.

Use these moments to practice your networking skills. Chat about what you do, ask others about their journey, and just listen. You don't need to dominate the conversation – just show genuine interest. Some of the best insights I've ever had were from casual chats on retreats.

And here's a big tip: don't limit yourself to only talking to the people you came with. That's such an easy trap to fall into, especially in group travel. Instead, stretch outside your comfort zone. Greet other travellers at the resort. Strike up a chat with someone new. You never know who you might meet – maybe the gold nugget of the trip is waiting outside your circle.

Be helpful. Be generous. Share your thoughts and ideas with others. And when that lightbulb moment hits – because trust me, it will – grab your phone, open your Notes app, and jot it down. Just bullet points. Don't overcomplicate it. You're not writing a book in that moment – you're simply capturing inspiration before it disappears into thin air.

6. Reflect and stay in touch

You've had the retreat. You're home. But the journey isn't over – this is actually one of the most important steps. Because what you do after the trip determines whether it was just a feel-good memory or a real turning point in your life.

Start by pulling out that piece of paper where you wrote down your intention before the retreat. Re-read it. Reflect on it. Did you have a breakthrough moment? Did your intention shift or deepen? Now's the time to take action on those ideas and insights while the energy is still fresh.

Don't wait. Momentum fades fast, so jump into implementing even just one or two things straight away. That excitement you felt when the idea landed? Use it. That spark is telling you something.

And here's a big one – stay in touch. Some of the strongest, longest-lasting friendships and business connections I've made came from a single trip together. There's something about being in a different place, away from the day-to-day, that creates deep, genuine bonds.

Continue the relationships you built – follow people on socials, send a quick message to say how much you enjoyed their company, or even organise a catch-up if you live nearby. And if you're in different states or countries, don't be afraid to travel to see each other. You shared something special. That kind of connection is worth nurturing.

You'll always have that trip as your anchor – that shared experience that bonds you. So check in, update your new friends on the progress you've made from the ideas you talked about. It keeps the energy alive and deepens the connection.

And if certain people really stood out to you, think about how you can keep that going. Maybe even plan your next getaway together. Relationships need time to grow—and retreats are just the beginning.

7. Do it again and again and again

One of my favourite things to see in my calendar – and I highly recommend this – is my next trip already booked. Whether it's a personal holiday, a solo retreat, or a group getaway like *Bond and Beyond*, there's something powerful about knowing it's locked in. It gives you something to look forward to and keeps your motivation and inspiration flowing year-round.

If you're attending an annual retreat with a particular community or company, or you're the one planning it, get ahead of the game. Have the next destination chosen, get your quotes sorted, and start planting the seed with attendees before the current retreat even ends.

For those who had an amazing time, there's no better moment to say 'yes' to the next one. I always offer an Uber early bird special during the retreat itself, because that's when the energy is high, the bonds are fresh, and the memories are being made. And honestly, why wouldn't you lock it in early if you know you want to go again? Sure, there's a small risk with a non-refundable deposit, but chances are, you'll save big compared to booking later.

But more than that, it's about nurturing relationships and building something long-term. The best connections, collaborations, and ideas don't always happen overnight. They unfold over years, with repeated touchpoints, shared memories, and those intentional pauses from the everyday grind.

So keep the rhythm going. Keep investing in yourself, your growth, and your community. Make space to pause. And then? Innovate. Dream. Create. Connect. And do it all again.

Because life's too short to only have one amazing retreat. Why not have one every year?

My Big 3 Aha! Moments: What I Took Away from Bond and Beyond Bintan

For me, this trip was wonderful in a different way. My three biggest takeaways were:

1. 15 improvement ideas for next year's *Bond and Beyond* – I can't wait to put them in place.

2. The realisation I only want to work four hours per day, five days per week. Will start this one in the second half of this year when I return from three more trips I am going to in the meantime.

3. My retreat groups are my extended family as I don't have many blood relatives in Australia, so I gather people from all over the world to holiday and have fun with as I did when I was a child back home in Macedonia.

Bond and Beyond Bintan Family 2025.

Our White Night with love heart pins in our hair.

Nat meeting a Colugo for the first time (also known as a 'Flying Lemur'). Nat pronounced it in a French accent rather than 'LEE-mur' and everyone laughed at her!

CHAPTER 2 - VIVIENNE MASON

JUST IMAGINE

*"Some painters transform the sun into a yellow spot,
others transform a yellow spot into the sun."*
(Pablo Picasso)

It's 5:30am and I am waking up to the sound of birds and insects that are calling in the new day, the waves lap on the beach and it is time to take a moment to be grateful for the new dawn, a pause before busy, a breath before breaking the peace.

It is time to move at a slower pace, at one with the rhythms of the ocean. The moon is high in the sky and the colours are muted, soft lilacs and greys.

I walk to the rock boulders, they sit in huddles at the end of the beach, not quite a circle. They have been here a long time having a conversation and I love their rounded shapes from constant weathering. Like sisters together, they are a family.

I make fresh footprints as I wander along the shoreline. Bare footed, from wet lush grass to soft sandy beach and warm sea water. The sensations are grounding me as I find my way in the semi-dark. I add my own prints to the ones a lizard has made on his night time meanders. I feel blessed that all is good in the world.

Every minute slower, every breath intended to heal and rejuvenate.

The sun slowly creeps up from the horizon and shimmers a golden path into the ocean, as if saying, 'This is the way', follow the golden reflections one step at a time. It is a warm welcome, accompanied by the crescent moon and the bright star Venus, gleaming in the morning sky. Meanwhile, the clouds billow upward, stretching toward the heavens, a reassuring sign that the day is beginning.

For me, this morning ritual of appreciation, taking in the scenery, awakening the senses, looking at the new textures and listening to the sounds, has been amazing. This is the pause I have been hoping for. The slow release of pent-up emotions, a settling down of the inner self, like a shaken snow globe. I am now in my calm space.

I have left behind my family and sadly, my beautiful cat Whitey, who passed away the Friday before I left. The sadness has been submerged just under the surface and needs time to dissolve. I miss him so much. I am hoping to heal his loss as it has ploughed up other feelings of grief that reside deep in the crevices. I acknowledge the sadness as it is part of life, but still it stings.

Love keeps me going, there is so much to be thankful for.

When Nat first mentioned the *Bond and Beyond* experience, I was hesitant, as I have my job working with all our authors and I thought that we're too busy with the constant stream of emails. But I have been surprised. The Universe has aligned and allowed me time to enjoy the company of my team and these lovely authors, who are loving this time together. Getting to know them more personally and seeing what beautiful gifts they share with one another is a blessing.

My daily routine is one of gratitude as I know it is best to work on your mindset first thing in the morning and set the intention for the day.

I have also been feeding the inner artist by absorbing the colours and textures and it now bubbles within me like a bottle of Champagne waiting to be uncorked and I can't wait to celebrate this on the canvas, in my writing and in my life.

My higher self is telling me that work life balance is within my reach, I just need to create it and trust in the process. This is me being ME.

On day one of the workshop, the authors introduced themselves and told a little bit about their journey to become an author and their big **why**. This was a very moving experience, and I felt an instant connection with each of them. How wonderful to have this opportunity to connect and support one another in this space.

We worked through our questions in the workbook and each day a little voice was telling me to re-visit 'Onion Girl' – the metaphor in my first book.

Onion Girl was urging me to strip off the layers again and explore new themes of what it is like to 'pause' and see things from a new perspective. A transition was in motion, so I felt I better go with the flow.

My first book was about my perimenopause and my unintentional break away from family. I escaped to Europe, leaving my kids and husband behind. I had to find myself again. Not wanting to be a mother or a worker, my daily life was tough working a stressful job, dealing with sleepless nights and hot sweats. Irritability was my middle name, and my Lamia snake was uncoiling ready to strike.

Men-o-*pause* felt like the right thing to do at the time, so I headed to my mother's home in the UK countryside. My bag was heavy with the guilt and shame of a mother that chose to leave her husband and children behind. I was off on a three-month adventure, but it felt wrong. But to stay would mean I would have to endure more pain from my emotional and physical storm.

My profound moment came on day two of the conference sessions when I realised that I am still peeling my onion, and I have so much to share. The wisdom I have learnt on self-preservation needs to be shared to encourage women going through their own menopausal journey; to let them know it is a gift – a beautiful transformation.

An opportunity to embrace the third chapter of their womanhood and cross the bridge. On the other side is freedom to live, to explore and to share in their journey of hope. Find time to take a well-deserved 'pause' in their life, on their own terms. To be alone for a short while to totally rest and recuperate.

A 'pause' should be factored into every woman's life. Just imagine if you knew at some point during your menopause you were going on a lovely holiday, a special time away, an opportunity to grow and explore. I would love to see this on every woman's bucket list and hear them saying, 'When I am in perimenopause, I am going to the Greek Islands to explore ancient ruins and goddesses or go on a three-month adventure around Australia!'

One word has come up a lot during this retreat is **transition**. Moving from one state to the next and it is within this space, the gap between the ebb and flow, that magic happens. The pause between each breath is sacred as new possibilities rise up and it is in perfect timing that we all expand and move forward.

I am never tired of making new connections with the other authors as they are all wonderful, their kindness shines through their eyes and it has been a great experience hanging out with them all. I love getting to know each one on a deeper level, to connect, and I can see the potential that each of them holds. With so many new ideas and a-ha! moments, I know that this group of authors has so much to give and I am truly thankful to be part of their journey.

As the Publications Manager, I get to read a lot of personal stories, of life, love and loss, of the vulnerable experiences and the triumph over adversity. The themes are wonderfully moving, and I feel privileged to be a part of an author's journey. Each individual adds their voice to the world and brings new awareness, whether it be on personal adversity, or overcoming illness, or an entrepreneur change-maker – the author's gift of their story is a poignant one and will help so many people.

It also helps that I love to read so many books in one year! I sometimes get asked if I get sick of reading and I always answer, 'No way.'

To read so many books and to help them on their publishing journey is something that I never tire of. Even though it's busy – with over 60 books in process at this time – there is always time to help them each step of the way as it can be overwhelming and I am their hand held tight.

I will admit I am drawn to the artistic talents in the retreat group, as this is where I get my inspiration, share my loves and joy for all things creative and listen out for ideas. Diving deep into art expressions is what I like to do most, and I know I need to make the time to scratch this insatiable itch. Nat says, 'What gets scheduled, gets done' – and I know I have been bad at letting other priorities get in the way of my art practice and I realise how much of a priority my art and creativity needs to be right now. This retreat has made me realise that I need to make this a high priority again.

From the early morning sunrise walk I have a new set of colours in my head, and I want to let them loose on the canvas. I have promised myself to set time aside each week for painting and exploring the abstract textures as this is my happy space, it is when I am completely myself and where I find self-exploration so fulfilling. I would encourage anyone to do this, find the thing that makes you happy and do it – even if it means saying 'no' to the people you love.

All my life I have put people first, above myself as this is in my DNA. My nature is to help others and anyone who asks. I love meeting my friends and family, to hear all their news. I am a social butterfly flitting from one flower to the other. But I get very sad when I haven't had time to express myself and find meaning in my surroundings. This has been a big theme during the *Bond and Beyond Retreat* and I must get back to it.

The problem is I don't find art classes very stimulating anymore, as they are not offering what I want. Maybe it is time to create my own workshops and abstract, intuitive art classes? Now *that* is an idea seed planted from this retreat, and I am keen to see how it grows.

Lately, my biggest question has been whether I can truly create the right work-life balance that allows me to nurture my creative side while staying connected to nature. I often struggle to shift my mindset from project management to creative endeavours, and as a result, I tend to put off making time for artistic pursuits.

I know I need to push past these bad habits, as I fear not fulfilling my artistic dreams. It's clear I need to prove to myself that I can have both – the structure of my work and the freedom to create. The key is to plan it into my life and stop making excuses. I realise I've been holding myself back, and it's time to carve out space in my schedule for what matters most.

I can plan a weekend of painting and even book myself into a getaway destination. I now have a goal to buy some new canvases for my new project and add my tiny treasures for interest and texture. These are the earrings that have lost their twin, and I love how I can repurpose them from my history jewellery, which includes my mother's bits and bobs, along with the pebbles and shells, and small shiny objects.

After my mother passed away during the pandemic, I held onto many of her jewellery pieces, knowing one day they would find a place in my abstract art. Each item carries its own story, making the art feel more personal. A little bit of me, and a little bit of her, will go a long way.

The group activities have been a lot of fun and the *Club Med* whole operation seamless, with a great number of set changes bumping in tables outside for a garden dinner, or poolside show or party at the beach, then packing it all away.

We have so many activities, it is hard to choose one. But for me the best part of this retreat is wallowing in the ocean, floating in the crystal sea water, watching schools of fish dart about my feet and chatting to the authors.

The sea is my happy place where I can truly relax and unwind, with the added bonus of sharing stories and laughs with the authors. Simply floating about on my own, I feel truly blessed to be part of the ocean, this big expanse connecting all the lands around the globe fills me with a sense of awe.

Some of the best conversations with our lovely authors have happened in the water – laughing at jokes, sharing ideas and life experiences. It's been pure magic, making happy memories that will last a lifetime.

One night during the retreat, I found myself wading into the ocean with Luba. We spent over an hour floating and chatting, searching for a deeper spot but staying close enough to shore – because honestly, who knows what creatures are out there and I wasn't keen on becoming a shark's dinner!

I loved slipping away from the noise of the party, letting the happy sounds fade into the distance, and feeling the cool water wash away the sticky heat. Our conversation wandered from topic to topic, easy and real, and somewhere between the laughter and the waves, we truly connected. I felt so content, so grateful – a moment of pure peace and joy that I'll carry with me.

Another cherished memory is the karaoke night when Nat and Julie performed a duet of *Don't Go Breaking My Heart* by Elton John and Kiki Dee. They were the first to take the stage, setting the tone for a night full of uninhibited singing and laughter. It was so much fun watching Nat, who was always just a bit off-key, but completely immersed in the joy of the moment, having the best time without a care in the world.

Recently, I have been thinking about my transition into retirement as my husband has taken a well-earned break and so naturally, our conversations veer towards what retirement would look like for us as a couple.

My inner voice is saying there are so many more adventures to go on with Nat and the team and this retreat has given me even more reason to be a part of the author experience. I feel we all have so much to give each other and allow time to grow. I do realise that I am older than a lot of the authors here, but I don't feel my age. However, I am not getting any younger and so making the right decision towards retirement is important to me.

Life is short and so many of us suffer from ill health before our time is complete and I don't want to be that person who puts things off. My own father died at 63 years (my age next birthday) and this makes me nervous! Will I create all my dreams before my life is over?

Having this time away has really made me think on a deeper level and ask the big questions.

I believe in perfect timing of the Universe and so have been looking for little tell-tale signs and following the golden path of the sunrise each morning. Step by step, I am on my way – it's all in the journey.

I once asked, 'Where are all the wise men in the world?' To be honest, I have only found a few who can truly share their wisdom from the heart. But wise women are everywhere, and this retreat has reminded me of the true wisdom of women. And that is to share and encourage one another, hold space to express ourselves and love our differences. We are all unique and together, we are strong.

If I were to give one word of advice to the younger version of myself, it would be to stop feeling guilty about taking time off. Having a break from your family is necessary for your peace of mind, your health and happiness, as it creates space for growth and transition – to be who you are meant to be. When I am so busy with my work and life, I feel like I am holding my breath, and it is only when I take a pause, can I truly breathe out and let go of all the pent-up emotion. A great big sigh is a welcome release.

I am finally here. This is the moment. I am fully awake, recharged and at peace. My mind is clear and in full appreciation of every minute I am blessed with.

This retreat was a perfect time to be away from family, and gather my thoughts, work through my new grief from the loss of Whitey and plan a future that feeds my creative spirit.

Without this break, I would have kept moving in the same direction, but without the new perspective that new ideas can bring. This new inspiration is what I have needed and the words 'just imagine' kept popping into my head.

These two words created the open space, a door was opened and a new horizon beckoned me. I followed the trail of the golden pathway from the morning sunrise and now the next steps are down to me to take. I now have renewed enthusiasm and energy to go and make art, write my books and explore the offerings of my own workshops. This has been the gift of the retreat.

I encourage anyone to take a 'pause' and decompress. Life events happen to us, and everyone needs space to process the many challenges. The gift of time away for yourself is essential. Be kind to yourself, and let your inner voice tell you what you need for your soul.

Your purpose is to be the Becoming, the journey back to the I AM presence.

You are already enough. You are unique in your gifts and taking time to develop them is wonderful.

Just Imagine!

Love, Vivi

My team buddy Julie and I, love our cheeky time together!

Nat and I renewing our 'work wife' vows again 5 years later!

A morning sunrise on Bintan beach, so peaceful.

Reflections on the lily pond, art inspiration right there...

About Vivienne Mason

Vivienne Mason is the Publications Manager with the *Ultimate 48 Hour Author* team, supporting over 100 authors each year on their publishing journey. With a deep passion for helping people find their voice, she brings decades of experience in the book industry, including retail management, publishing data analysis and authorship.

Vivienne wrote *Onion Girl*, her 'femoir' about her menopausal journey. Originally from Hampshire, UK, she has lived in Melbourne with her Aussie husband and their two sons for over 20 years. A creative at heart, she enjoys basket weaving, abstract art and holds a lifelong love of history and storytelling.

tinyurl.com/oniongirlbook

CHAPTER 3 - JULIE FISHER

OPPORTUNITIES

"Opportunity is not about luck. It is about the ability to recognise the opportunity when it appears, then, GRAB IT WITH BOTH HANDS."
(Remez Sasson)

As I arrived at Melbourne Airport, the nerves and excitement were building fast. This was my second overseas trip and I couldn't wait to embark on this journey for our *Bond and Beyond Retreat* with our team and some of our authors.

I felt instant relief when I learned that Vivi had arrived at the airport at exactly the same time as me because I was unsure of the steps to check in. Even though I had done this once before, the nerves were overwhelming.

Everything went off without a hitch and before we knew it, we were boarding the plane on our way to Singapore.

I couldn't wait to see this country and all the 'pretty' as I had seen so many amazing photos from friends who had been there before. This country looked amazing online through all these photos and this time, I was going to experience it.

Singapore didn't disappoint with the lush, green gardens and beautiful flowers around every corner. This country was so clean, the transport so safe and well organised and the sights were just breathtaking.

One of my favourite nights in Singapore was when we met our author, Quan. It was so lovely to meet her face to face, get to know her more and let her take us to her favourite place to eat. We went through alley ways and up some stairs to a place that tourists wouldn't know about. We shared a delicious feast together and enjoyed great conversations.

Another stand out day was when we hosted our half day workshop to a room of 60 budding authors wanting to learn more about publishing their books. Sitting in the room, listening to Nat speak, I was taken back to the first I met her when I was one of the people in the room, eager to learn more.

That day was the beginning of the amazing journey I am now on, and I will never forget how I felt, full of nerves and almost walking out of the room. I'm so glad I didn't because I love where my books have taken me and working for Nat is incredible.

In Singapore, as Nat was delivering the workshop, I was given the opportunity to stand in front of this crowd of people and share my authoring journey, as well as the work I'm now doing in the disability sector.

OPPORTUNITIES

That day, I became an international speaker!

As I spoke, I looked at the faces in the audience and loved seeing how connected they were to my story. Sharing our stories is so important because they create connection, build empathy and help others feel seen and understood.

I love sharing our journey and hearing the impact it has on others and I am so grateful for the day I met Nat and all the things that have come over the last six years through the learning from her.

Travelling is also one of the wonderful opportunities I get to experience working with our *Ultimate 48 Hour Author* team.

Singapore was the beginning of this journey and once we had spent four days there, it was time to head to an island for our week-long retreat with some of our authors, including Luba and Sydney from the USA and Zoe from Canada.

On Saturday, we headed to the ferry for an hour-long trip to the island of Bintan which is in Indonesia. Checking our bags in like you do at an airport; we were all filled with excitement and ready for our adventure.

Meeting our authors face to face after many years on *Zoom* calls was great. There were hugs all around and the beginning of many conversations that were to come over the coming week.

We boarded the ferry, and the chatter was constant as we waited to see where we were going to spend this time together. I couldn't wait to get there, and the anticipation was buzzing through my body.

We arrived at the island, but there was one more transport we needed to take to get to the *Club Med* resort. We got on board a bus, and we soon filled the air with chatter and excitement for the week ahead. All of a sudden, our theme song for the retreat, *'APT'* was playing loudly and we instantly joined in singing and dancing!

The other passengers were smiling, laughing and joining in. Most of us love this song and were singing at the top of our voices. The ones who didn't quite like it would come to like it by the end of our week.

As we arrived at *Club Med*, we were greeted with many smiling faces, people waving and greeting us filled with happiness. It was like the time we arrived at *Club Med* in Thailand the year before. Their happiness built our excitement for the week even more.

I went straight to the balcony as we arrived and saw the breathtaking views of palm trees and the magnificent beach that was going to be ours. The air was hot and humid, and we were ready to begin our *Bond and Beyond Retreat*.

Being in the publishing team of *Ultimate 48 Hour Author* brought me this experience and I was looking forward to getting to know our authors more, bonding with the team and learning from the workshops that Nat had planned for us. She always gives us such amazing and valuable information and I never get tired of hearing it.

It was just the beginning of our adventure and we were filled with so much excitement.

Settling in on the first day, we found our rooms, unpacked and chatted with our roommate if we had one. I shared a room with Carmen, and even though I had met her a couple times before, I was looking forward to getting to know her even more.

She's been such a great support for me, even though we have only known each other for a short time. I'm looking forward to learning more from her as our friendship grows.

After a weekend of settling in, enjoying delicious meals and of course, cocktails, we were ready to start our workshops. The workbooks we had were awesome and over the next couple of days, we worked through them, each of us contributing to the conversations giving each other ideas and support.

A room full of eager women, it was hard on day one to stop the chatter, so a beach ball was introduced on day two and this worked so well. As each person was ready to speak, they received the ball, and nobody could talk while they were speaking. It was such an awesome idea that gave everyone their chance to contribute to the group.

Our new invention to keep the focus on the person speaking: 'Beach Ball Mode'.

These three days were so good and insightful. Some of the informaion I have learned before, and I also learned some new things, but it's always good to go over things again especially in today's world where there are always so many changes and tools coming to us. Having the contributions of everyone in the room was beneficial too and I think sharing raw and honestly helped many of us who sometimes feel stuck.

For me, I am doing many amazing things in the disability sector from my books, but there is always the want to do more for the community. I have some great ideas but keep them locked away in fear of judgement. It seems silly that I still feel like this six years after publishing my first book, but it's still there.

That pesky imposter syndrome sits on my shoulders quite often and after the three days of learning, my biggest takeaway was to trust myself. I know what I have to do and with the learning from the workshops, I learned more about how to do that.

This was a great moment for me and seemed to be the theme for the week, and that is to step outside my comfort zone and do what I need to do. Test myself and push myself.

Spending time with everyone also showed me that when listening to their journeys and stories of resilience. I don't think I got along with anyone better than anyone else over the week because everyone was so individual and each conversation quite different.

I loved being able to spend time with everyone and continue learning, as well as bonding with them all and having some fun.

I did spend quite a bit of time on my own which I also really enjoyed. I think with all the busy I experience in my life, I needed that quiet time to walk or just sit and enjoy the surroundings. The simple things are sometimes the best and what we need the most. When we are busy, we do tend to forget this and push it to the side.

The activities at the resort were action packed and I loved being able to try the trapeze again. The first time I did it was when we were in Phuket in 2024 and when I came off, my whole body was shaking with fear and adrenaline. I loved doing it that time, but I didn't think I would ever do it again.

When I saw the trapeze at Bintan, I immediately knew I wanted to do it again to see if the fear would subside. Carmen bravely said she would do it with me and I loved sharing this experience with her.

We headed to our room not expecting the trapeze to be open due to thunder, but to our surprise, it was, and we looked at each other and Carmen said, 'C'mon, let's do it!'

I was scared, but more excited to try it again.

Climbing the ladder is scary in itself because it isn't very wide, it is straight up and down, and it does have a slight wobble to it. As you climb, you think you're almost to where you need to be and then you look to see and realise you still have quite a bit of climbing to do. But, up you go.

When you reach the top, you need to place all your trust in the person that is there waiting to get you on the trapeze and that is because of the way you have to stand and reach out for the bar. Stepping forward, holding onto a bar on the left, bending your knees and leaning forward ready to grab the bar as they hold you by the strapping around your waist. Of course, they also strap you up to a harness so even if you did fall, you wouldn't hurt yourself.

The bar comes forward and you grab. It is heavy but you hold on. Then she tells you to let go of the bar on the left and hold the bar with two hands. It is so scary letting go but once you do, you have both hands on the bar.

Next is to hop off the platform and swing. You hear 'hop' and off you go squealing with delight in the feat you have just conquered. Back and forth a few times and then it's time to let go and fall onto the net. This is also scary but once you do it, you hit the safety of the net and... YOU'VE DONE IT!

Letting go on the Trapeze in Bintan... Woohoo!

This time was still scary for me, but my body wasn't shaking as much as the first time.

Carmen climbed up and had her turn and was so pleased she did it. We were very proud of ourselves.

Before the week was over, I wanted to do it again and I did. This time, even though the fear was still there, my body wasn't shaking at all when I finished. I don't know if I'll ever do the trapeze again, but I'm so glad I conquered that fear. It was always something I'd seen and wanted to do.

The other activities at the resort were great and I took a turn to try most of them. Having fun going out on the boat for snorkelling was lovely. I didn't pass the swim test so they didn't let me snorkel, but I enjoyed sitting at the back of the boat with one of the guides talking to him about what his dreams were and about the things that I do. His dream was to come to Australia and work for a while and I told him he should do it. If it's something he wants, make sure he does it, because otherwise, he will always wonder what would have happened.

We saw some amazing fish while we sat at the back of the boat, so it was still a great activity to do and I loved watching Carmen enjoy the wonders of the ocean.

The foam party was a blast, and the golf driving range was fun — even though I am terrible at hitting a golf ball — and archery was great. I did it so much better than the first time I had tried it and managed to get 10 arrows out of 12 on target.

The monkeys were in full cheek mode at the archery activity, climbing along the fence, peeking out from under the netting and throwing down huge leaves from the palm trees. We were told that at times, they sit on top of the target.

We were also blessed to see a very unusual animal called a colugo hugging one of the palm trees one night. A very different animal that is also known as the 'Flying Lemur'. It's nocturnal and glides between the palms foraging for food at night. Nat and Felicity caught one gliding between the trees one night... Another special moment.

Another highlight for Vivi, Zoe, Chris and I was doing a tour through the mangroves. Such an amazingly beautiful area filled with wonderful history, stories and animals. We were lucky to see some snakes, a lizard and some gorgeous butterflies. It really was a beautiful experience, and I'm so pleased we were able to do it.

This trip also gave me a chance to meet some other people from around the world. One family stands out the most as we talked many times over a few days. They asked me many questions about our story and the work I'm doing and told me about their daughter who they're very worried about.

Their daughter is undergoing assessments to get some answers, but currently, she self-harms and has some awful scars on her arm. Her mum told me she understood what I was talking about when I spoke about stares from others towards Darcy. She told me she hated the way people looked at her daughter in a judgemental way and she hoped that I would get to meet her.

I did meet their daughter and what a beautiful girl she is. We spoke for quite a while with her asking me questions and talking openly about herself harming. I didn't stare at her; I listened and answered her questions as she asked them.

It came back to me a couple days later that her mum wanted to tell her to meet me but knew her daughter would say no. She was delighted when she heard we met and after speaking with her daughter, she said my conversation with her was already life-changing.

Cup full right there. It's so important to continue sharing our stories and create those much-needed conversations. You never know what may come from it.

Spending time with our team was special, too. From working alongside Vivi and chatting about our adventure to an Anzac Day service on the beach with everyone, karaoke with Nat (so much fun), watching the Anzac Day football match and lots of wonderful conversations. It's very special and I'm always grateful to be part of this amazing group of people.

Trying new things and making plans for the future were all highlights for me with this trip away and I would encourage everyone to do a trip like this if given the opportunity. You will come away with a full heart, new friendships and lots of learning.

This retreat gave me time to anchor, look at what I'm doing and learn about how I can do the things I want to do with my job and with the work I do in the disability sector. I am about to launch my fifth book sharing our journey with Darcy through the teenage years and even though this book isn't published yet, I can already see new things I'll be able to do to support the community.

This experience gave me many opportunities...to become an international speaker, to learn from others and to trust myself and push that imposter syndrome out of the way, so I can continue to do great things.

Opportunity is there for us at any given moment, but it's when we embark on something like this retreat, that we really see it and embrace it.

I'm so grateful for everything that I've learned and all the things I'm doing, and I look forward to more opportunities coming my way, so I can keep supporting others and continue to learn and grow.

Stunning beach at Bintan and a great space to have 'me' time. Something I enjoyed regularly during this trip.

The foam party was such a blast, dancing to music and getting covered in bubbles.

OPPORTUNITIES

My second overseas trip and I'm so grateful for all the opportunities I have been given. I cannot wait until the next one.

About Julie Fisher

Julie Fisher is a proud mum, step mum, wife, carer, speaker and author.

Inspired by her son Darcy, who lives with Down syndrome, Julie shares her family's journey through her books *The Unexpected Journey*, *The Magic of Inclusion*, *From the Hearts of Mums* and *Big School*.

Passionate about raising awareness and creating acceptance in the community, she works alongside families of children with disabilities and regularly speaks on inclusion and the carer experience.

Julie's heartfelt advocacy has made global connections, with Darcy becoming an ambassador for several inclusive organisations.

Through storytelling, Julie aims to create a kinder world where every person is valued. Contact Julie at *hello@juliefisher.com.au*

CHAPTER 4 - WENDY TREVARTHEN

FINDING COURAGE BEYOND THE WAVES

"In the sea's embrace, courage calms, connections deepen and we become a powerful ripple in something greater."
(Wendy Trevarthen)

Attending the *Bond and Beyond Retreat* in Bintan was a non-negotiable for me. I wanted to experience Indonesia, be a part of being with the team and also meet new authors I hadn't yet encountered in my three-year journey with the *Ultimate 48 Hour Author* team. I was excited to board the ferry in Singapore after a weeklong holiday. Meeting everyone as they trickled to the ferry terminal was exciting and to meet them all in person and not through a *Zoom* call was surreal.

I knew the ferry trip would be smooth, and even if it was going to be choppy, I cope pretty well with the rocking of any boat. I wasn't anticipating any rough weather, and I didn't experience any seasickness at all during the crossing. Mind you, I'm used to riding the waves!

When I initially heard that we were catching the ferry to Bintan, I had images of being squashed into an antiquated junk, fighting for space and wishing the trip was over before it began. I was pleasantly surprised to see that the ferry was like the *CityCats* in Brisbane, reassuring me that all would be okay.

Buzzing Bus Vibes

Prior to leaving on the ferry from Singapore at the *Club Med* booth, we all were given envelopes and donned the bracelet which held our room key. We each followed suit, tagging our luggage for pick up and transport to the Island.

The excitement on the bus varied. Some people sat quietly, while others chatted. The music on the bus really put us in the mood – we knew we were going to be a high-energy group with lots of shared experiences. There was much chitter chatter with "Ooo's" and "Ahhh's" when we arrived at the gate for *Club Med*.

The lush green landscape and manicured gardens were stunning full of reds, oranges of both leaves and flowers. The lipstick palms in front of the spa were well established and gorgeous.

Warm Island Welcome

Bintan itself – the resort – was a little older than our *Club Med Phuket* experience last year. The staff were lovely. We could see them greeting us with warm welcomes, big smiles, and always with a courteous greeting. Once they learned your name, it was a 'Good morning, Miss Wendy!'

When we saw the pool area and the main bar, we knew we were in for a glorious seven days ahead. The accommodation units were spread out along the beach front, three levels over a terraced landscape. It was a good workout going up several flights of stairs (no lifts unfortunately) to the gym/sports area, which had many courts of every racket game imaginable. The huge drainage either side of the walkway was a reminder of the tropical downpours that the country often experiences.

Our room was gorgeous, decorated with colour and vibrancy, a balcony area overlooking the grassland and then the beautiful beach, where my roommate, Vivi, and I could view the sunrise each morning.

One day when I had planned to do archery at the very end of the sports area during a sudden onset thunderstorm, sirens sounded, alerting everyone that the storm was less than four kilometres away. The archery was postponed for 20 minutes, and the eventual outcome is that I did not go back to do this activity.

Space for Self

Prior to the retreat, I was deep in work and family mode, not taking much time for myself – even though I was carving out space in my day for self-care, exercise and nutrition. Coming to the retreat allowed me to step away from my busy routine and experience the tranquillity of the environment. I felt the more-than-usual humid weather, and I knew when I agreed to this experience that I'd be blending work and pleasure. It was a chance for me to sit with where I was at, clear some space, and look forward to creating opportunities for myself.

The connections with the other authors also evoked a curiosity inside me, expanding my thoughts into what could be, rather than what was in the past. I know that I have a lot of experience and wisdom (indeed my nickname during the retreat was 'Wise Wendy'), however my lack of confidence to speak out my thoughts and ideas is still one aspect of my skillset that I work on daily. The retreat allowed me time to explore what this meant for me.

Water Brings Clarity

There's just something about water. Being a Cancerian, I've always felt connected to water. I've always wanted to live near water – and I'm grateful I do. Most mornings, I walk along the waterfront with friends, enjoying those peaceful moments. But in Bintan, being in the water itself gave me space to appreciate the environment and tune into the sounds of nature – the birds, the trees, and the waves – like the rhythm of a heartbeat, ebbing and flowing, giving us life and energy.

Most mornings found me rising early and greeting the sun with a morning swim, the water was shallow, calm and felt such a beautiful way to start each day. Floating on my back and watching the change in the skyscape was exhilarating. After drying off, I headed to the dining room, and slowly greeted the other group members for a chat about the day ahead.

On Anzac Day, eight of us gathered at dawn to pay our respects and listening to the last post. This made me think of home, my military family members past and present, with pride and gratitude. It especially helped me reflect on my parents, as they often holidayed in the tropics and lived in Malaya (as it was once called) before my older sister and I were born. I imagined how their lives must have been back then in the mid 1950s, enjoying the Army life in that country. That morning, I also thought of my son, Will, who I usually spend Anzac Day with during the Sydney Anzac Day march. I was delighted later that day to receive a photo of him in his uniform with his girlfriend and felt joy as I could see the happiness in his eyes.

It's creating space such as this that allows us to have gratitude for the memories that you have and the association that the day and the environment brings for you.

Rewriting Rejection Narrative

Have you ever carried rejection for so long you mistook it for part of who you are?

The key moment for me during the retreat was shifting many thoughts around personal rejection. To give you some background – nursing had been my career for 36 years. When I created my two books and developed the offerings from them, I still carried a cloud of rejection from my nursing days.

I was a strong advocate for families and clients when I worked and when I spoke up or out, it was often superseded by others' thoughts and feelings – ones that didn't always prioritise the patient. I internalised that as personal rejection. I now know that the staff were not rejecting me; they were fearful of the truth and I was a reminder to them of that truth.

Courage Breakthrough Moment

I've since learned that there were many contextual reasons my voice wasn't heard. The breakthrough I had during this retreat was in transforming those feelings of rejection into a deep recognition that I hold enormous courage within me.

Courage to move forward.

Courage to see facts before emotion.

Courage to meet people where they are and put them first.

This was a true mindset shift. What would it take for you to reconnect with your courage?

Even though I'd written and reflected on courage before, it hit me like an anvil – **courage** is what I need to focus on. Courage is more powerful than rejection. And I realised I'd been carrying that rejection daily. People might not have noticed, as I come across as quietly confident, but deep inside, that rejection from my nursing past – and other parts of my life – was holding me back. What I've now recognised is the power of my courage, and that I can call on it when I keep my purpose front of mind to guide me through those tough moments.

Creativity Awakens Self

Among the group, there were all sorts of personalities – some strong, others quietly confident. I found there was great depth in the creativity and spirituality and that opened a question for me about my own creative side. I do have one, although it's more connected to music. I'd like to return to that musical mindset, because it's through music that I connect with stories – the lyrics, the tunes, the words. A few musical experiences during the retreat really touched my heart and reminded me to open space in my personal time to foster that creativity of music.

Music Unlocks Meaning

Music, for me, unlocks deep emotions that have stood the test of time. During the Bintan retreat, we had many opportunities to listen to solo artists, other performers, and even enjoy the talent within our group when they shared their karaoke skills. The music itself is, of course, generation-dependent, but a lot of the older-style soft rock took me back to a time when I was growing up with my loving family around me. The lyrics and melodies stirred distant memories – songs you can sing word-for-word, even though you wouldn't normally think of them on your own.

Music touches deep within my soul and brings back joyous memories of family and connection. It grounds me in my identity and reminds me of who I truly am. Music is a beautiful medium that I hope to explore more in the future. I've made a promise to myself to rekindle my love for playing the flute and to embrace this creative side of me once again.

The Beauty of Finding Joy

The most joyful experience of all? Seeing lightbulbs go off in the other authors' faces. I know that sounds external, but that's how I'm wired. I love seeing the epiphanies in other people's minds erupting. Personally, the joy came from creating the space to recognise my courage. I also felt the deep connection with water, as it was all around us and even beauty in the afternoon thunderstorms.

Time to Act

There are habits I want to change – particularly around procrastination when it comes to taking action for building my business around nursing transformations and transitions. I realised during the retreat that I've been wasting time, distracted by things that don't add value. Now, I'm focused on taking small actions each day. Completing my workday and using that time following to progress small, organised steps will help me gain momentum toward what I want to achieve.

Say 'Yes' Now

To anyone considering a retreat like this: do it. It's a chance to go to the next level, to see beyond your book and its original purpose. You'll open your mind to new opportunities, new collaborations and experience the wealth of knowledge in the room. Tapping into others' creativity – through conversation and connection – will give you strength to unlock potential you didn't even know you had. Saying 'Yes' could be your first step toward your own transformation.

Connections Fuels Courage

Writing a book can be isolating. And while I do enjoy solitude, I also recognise my need to connect with others. That conscious connection helps me step out of my comfort zone, to aspire, to learn and to understand myself more deeply. It creates those moments of courage that allow me to take micro-steps toward the goals I'm working to achieve.

The trip to Bintan (or anywhere) is time for you to create the space and watch as magic happens. Saying 'Yes' to you is a priority and provides you with the space for creativity and innovation.

Many thanks to Natasa Denman for having the vision for this retreat and for taking monumental action to make it happen. Being a team member allowed me to witness this from thought through to reality, and to see the hard work that went into delivering this for everyone.

Congratulations Nat, a beautiful, lifelong memory for all of us who participated.

Wendy

Stillness between sea and self.

Stories at the door of Raffles, he knows 'Everything!'

First toast, team bonding begins.

Anzac Day dawn service at the beach with the Last Post.

Yatzee challenge with the team.

About Wendy Trevarthen

Wendy is a passionate nurse with over 35 years' experience in public health, workforce development, education and leadership. She helps nurses navigate career transitions with confidence and clarity, so they can thrive in a changing healthcare world.

Wendy is also an author, global speaker and host of the *Your Nurse Voice Matters* podcast, where she shares practical tools and real stories to strengthen the nursing profession. She works part-time as a book strategist with the *Ultimate 48-Hour Author* team, where she enjoys the privilege of speaking with new authors every day about their ideas and goals.

Outside of work, Wendy is a 'fun Nan' to twin granddaughters and loves walking in nature as it rejuvenates her spirit.

https://www.healthyoptionsnow.org

CHAPTER 5 - CARMEN HILL

HOW ONE WOMAN'S 'YES' BECAME A LIFE-CHANGING LEGACY

"The power of now. The journey is the destination."
(Carmen Hill)

There are moments in life where your whole body says 'Yes' – sometimes it starts as a whisper, like a seed being planted and then when it is nurtured it becomes a full embodied, soulfully aligned 'Yes! Yes, Yes!'

Saying 'yes' to the Bintan *Bond and Beyond Retreat* was one of those moments.

I knew – with every fibre of my being – that this was more than a fun holiday adventure to rest and recharge. It was an investment.

An investment in my core values, the values I write about in my book, *Empowered Property Investing, From Divorce to Financial Freedom*, the pillars of my success.

It's an investment in *myself*, for I am my greatest asset! It's an investment in surrounding myself with successful people, proximity is power. It was an investment in the collaborative energy that is igniting more abundance and prosperity for my greatest mission: Empowering other women to invest in themselves.

When more women and children are educated.

Financially independent.

Safe.

Secure.

Valued, honoured respected and free, what a wonderful world it will be!

The journey is not about the destination, although Bintan is beautiful and serene, a true paradise on earth. The journey is the destination. It is about living fully, breathing in every moment, and evolving even more into the woman I am becoming. And in that spirit, I knew I wanted my family to be part of this adventure too.

It was a celebration of life, love, connection, and legacy.

Gratitude Anchored in Family

Before I even boarded the plane, my heart was overflowing with gratitude.

To my Dad and his partner, affectionately known as Aunty Lynn, thank you for lovingly caring for our little dachshund puppy, Tootsie, making this trip possible.

To my beautiful Mum, who journeyed with Beau and me to Singapore a week early – creating once-in-a-lifetime memories we'll cherish forever – and then returned to care for Beau and Tootsie while I was in Bintan.

To Poppy Pete and Nona Gail, who celebrated Easter and took Beau on bike rides while I made further investments in our family legacy.

To the *LEAP Centre* – my workplace as a paediatric occupational therapist – thank you for your flexibility and support. Your belief in my growth allows me to keep serving children with special needs while nurturing my mission of philanthropy for women and children.

A huge thank you as well to my investment partners – *Invest Logic, Soho, and Infinite Wealth* – for the financial opportunities that make this beautiful life possible.

These blessings are a reflection of the investments I've made in every area of life – and I rejoiced with my family as Singapore gifted us with surreal, 'pinch me' moments:

Standing in awe beneath the towering super-trees during the Garden Rhapsody light and music show, breathing in the misty mountain air of the Cloud Forest, marvelling at the world's tallest indoor waterfall, and being dazzled by the ever-changing blooms inside the Flower Dome.

We swam in rooftop pools, rode rollercoasters at *Universal Studios*, and shared breakfast with orangutans and wildlife at the *Singapore Zoo* – all before I even dipped my toes in the oceans of Bintan or flew high on the trapeze at *Club Med*.

Family first: Adventures with my mum Wilma and son Beau at the Singapore Zoo.

I'm so grateful and blessed to be living my best life:

Full of abundance.
Full of joy.
Full of love.
Fully on purpose.

Tears of joy welled in my eyes — the kind that feel like a prayer answered, a life aligned. I remember walking into the breakfast room one morning in Bintan and seeing Nat — I couldn't hold them back.

I embraced her tightly and, through my tears, reassured her they were tears of pure gratitude, joy, and awe for my life and this sacred occasion shared with her and our author community.

Tears of recognition that we were exactly where we were meant to be:

In the right place.
At the right time.
With the right people.
Creating a life-defining, sacred experience that will echo through our souls forever.

Reconnecting with the Power of Community

There is a divine grace that happens when women gather with a shared intention: to heal, to be whole and complete, to grow, to rise, and to celebrate the magnificent lives we are here to live.

At Bintan, I connected with the joy of the wholesome power of community.

I was so blessed to meet new people from all walks of life and share in the sense of belonging and honouring the power of our collective energy to rise together.

There was a beautiful harmony of quality time to be still, pampered at the day spa, present in the calm breeze of the ocean waves rolling onto the shore, reflective and becoming. It is so refreshing to know as we walk this journey of life, we are together to lift each other higher and to celebrate in all the glory of this richness of life.

That truth ran like life force energy through my body during every inner circle mastermind, and every dance party under the stars.

It was a soul homecoming – a reminder that together, we are infinite.

And that beautiful lesson came with an equally powerful companion:

The importance of preparation. Energetically and practically.

My property mentor taught me:

'Be in state, it is like setting an intention for what you want to attract and if you're early, you're on time.'

For me, these lessons echoed throughout the retreat. Nat's theme of 'Love' unified us all, in the T-shirts she created for us, our heart-themed and white night dinner parties and our playful love heart hair accessories. Sometimes, it is the little things that bring so much joy, and a sense of belonging.

Our branded merch for the retreat – check out the front cover of us wearing them!

HOW ONE WOMAN'S 'YES' BECAME A LIFE-CHANGING LEGACY

Nat and Carmen wearing the 'Love' theme hair accessories.

It's about the gift of being fully prepared, and fully present.

It was about being attuned to the rhythm of life and honouring the sacredness of divine timing.

Not rushed.
Not frantic.
But deeply aligned.
Ready to receive.

No idea is fully formed and sharing in the ease and grace of creation is a beautiful way to enjoy life. I love that Nat shared with us that she was learning and refining as she went, and this is a powerful lesson in creation and achieving success: start and then refine.

Health Is Our Greatest Asset

Health is the foundation of everything, with it, everything becomes possible.

This retreat deepened my reverence for health – my physical health, my mental health, my social emotional health and my spiritual health and wellness.

Our physical health is the temple of the soul. It houses our energy, our joy, our vitality.

Our mental health and the language we choose to speak to ourselves, and others becomes the true north compass for making meaning of the life we live and living a life well lived.

And our spiritual connection to the greatest good, the infinite, the Universe as I like to call it, the most powerful essence there is – this is pure living.

I moved my body in ways that brought me so much joy:

Dancing on the beach.

Stretching into long, delicious yoga poses.

Floating, swimming, snorkelling and running into the water like a *Baywatch* babe.

Morning walks along the ocean shore, witnessing a new dawn.

Lifting weights in the gym and sharing laughter with Nat, Luba, and the aunties, and sharing a session with Lisa with her strength and passion as a personal trainer.

Each nourishing meal, each moment of rest, each expression of joy and song sung at karaoke, enriched my health and well-being, each moment of dance – it was all an investment in the temple of my well-being.

I nurtured my mental and emotional health, too. Mornings began with strength training and powerful affirmations that set me up to win the day. I reminded myself that the Universe has my back, that everything is always working out for my highest good. That I choose how I feel in any given moment.

My devotion to cultivating a positive, optimistic outlook and the practice of deep gratitude for the blessings in my life – the ease, the grace, the miracles.

This is the affirmation I speak, feel, and embody:

'I am galactically abundant, miraculously prosperous, worthy and deserving of the very best in life. I receive all the abundance the Universe has to offer me, and I receive it now with gratitude – for my greatest good and the greatest good of all.'

This mantra is more than words – it's an incantation that I embody. When I speak it with truth, it shifts my energy and calls in miracles. It reminds me that my vibrancy is my legacy and that I am committed to honouring and nurturing my health every single day.

Health is not just the absence of illness. It is energy. Clarity. Joy. Freedom.

It is our most valuable asset.

My health is my wealth.

The Journey Is the Destination

One of the most powerful transformations I've experienced was a deep, embodied realisation:

'The journey itself is the destination.'

Life isn't something we're racing toward.
It's not a finish line.
It's right here – in every breath, every laugh, every sunset, every tear.
In every act of courage.
In every moment of surrender.

At Bintan, I fell in love with *the moment*.
With being in it.
With celebrating it – instead of rushing through it to get somewhere else.

And nowhere was that more profound than at sunrise on Anzac Day, standing barefoot on the shores of Bintan.
Beside me: beautiful women from Australia, New Zealand, Canada and more.

Together, we created a simple, sacred ceremony on the beach – feet in the sand, hands on our hearts.

We remembered the bravery of the soldiers and nurses.
Those whose lives were lost at war.
Those whose stories must live on.
It was a powerful reminder:

We are the living prayers of those who came before us.

And peace – precious peace – is something to be honoured, protected, and nurtured every single day.

In that moment, my mind went to the War Memorial in Singapore.

I had visited with my mum and my son – a trip my dad had suggested before we left. As we read the names and ages etched into the stone, I felt the weight of history wrap around my heart.

So many were so young.
So many dreams, loves, and lives lost to the horrors of war.

We stood there – three generations – honouring them with our presence, our gratitude, our tears.

A solemn moment. A sacred one.

A deep bow to the nurses, the soldiers, the civilians – all who endured unimaginable suffering.

And a wave of gratitude that we live in peace.

Presence. Gratitude. Reverence.

That morning, as the sun kissed the sea and the breeze wrapped around us like a blessing, something anchored deeply in my soul:

This is what matters.
This is who I am.
This is the life I am here to live.

A life of celebration.
A life of remembrance.

A life of profound love for *this* moment — this beautiful, miraculous moment — and all the ones to come.

Soulful Connections and Sisterhood — Friends for Life

The true beauty of a retreat like this lies not only in the transformation within, but in the connections you create — with the souls you choose to walk alongside, and those who choose you in return.

With Luba, we spoke deeply about relationships — the importance of love, truth, harmony, and conscious partnership.

Her words carried an ancient wisdom that awakened something deep within me — a knowing of the love I'm calling in, and the soulful love I'm here to both give and receive.

Felicity, like a kindred spirit, shared her ceremony of inner marriage — the sacred union of yin and yang, the dance of masculine and feminine energies within and all around us.

It was a celebration of balance; a harmony that reminded me true empowerment comes from embracing both strength and softness. It felt like a blessing whispered directly to my soul.

Julie and Claire — their joy was contagious!

Their laughter, zest for life, and ability to connect with people of all ages, abilities, and cultures was pure humanity in motion.

Thank you to Julie, my roomie, for going first on the flying trapeze, and to Claire for inviting me to the traditional Indonesian wedding. My heart swelled watching her speak so gracefully in the native tongue — bridging worlds with love and respect.

HOW ONE WOMAN'S 'YES' BECAME A LIFE-CHANGING LEGACY

Flying high: Feel the fear and do it anyway!

It was a living testament to the power of connection, and the beauty of seeing and honouring each other's humanity.

And then, over breakfast with the Macedonian Aunties – hearing their stories of resilience, love, and community – I felt the ancient threads of womanhood weaving through time, linking us all.

Their fierce love for family, deep sense of belonging, and pride in tradition was humbling, inspiring, and deeply nourishing.

Honouring the Circle

I'm forever grateful to Natasa, who leads with fierce love and compassion. As Julie said, 'She's the best boss.'

Thank you for setting the sacred intention, creating the blueprint, and holding space for transformation to unfold – all while dancing up a storm, rocking your bikinis and playing with a beach ball.

Her heart, vision, and devotion to women's empowerment set the stage for miracles. And to her incredible team – Vivienne, Wendy and Julie – thank you for sharing your passion and purpose with us.

To Sydney, for the Moon Ceremony that reconnected us with the ancient rhythms of creation – a dance of cosmic energies that live within us all. I can't wait to see you again on our US trip in 2026.

To Alicia, for embodying compassion, forgiveness, and Christ consciousness – a reminder that faith and love walk hand in hand.

I was also reminded of the power of prayer in Singapore, when Mum didn't quite make it onto the train. My son and I prayed for her safety, and the alchemy we felt inspired us to act, reunite with her, and offer comfort and peace.

To Christine, for her vibrant wisdom and joyful living – a reminder that life is richest when fully harvested. I'm looking forward to the Elvis Festival in Parkes!

To Zoe, for her deep love of nature – the colugo sighting was incredible – and her insightful connection with the animal kingdom, reminding us we are part of something far greater than ourselves.

And to Lisa, for her strength, courage, and fierce devotion to health and vitality. Her voice, clear and powerful, inspired us all to rise and speak our truths.

Every woman carried a sacred gift.
Every interaction, a brushstroke on the masterpiece of our shared journey.

Celebrating Life, Love, and New Adventures

We soared high on the trapeze, belly-laughed through the foam bath, and danced our hearts out at the beach party, the garden party, and disco nights under the stars.

We indulged in a luxurious high tea at *Raffles Hotel Singapore* and basked in the abundance of *Club Med Bintan* – savouring dishes from around the world, tasting the exotic sweetness of mangosteen, getting pampered at the day spa, and unwinding on sun beds beneath the shade of tiki umbrellas.

Some of the unforgettable highlights included:

- Snorkelling among vibrant marine life – colourful fish, graceful eels, delicate sea urchins, and the crackling coral, all while the ocean kissed my skin with salty bliss.
- Relaxing massages at the day spa, accompanied by soulful conversations with fellow guests.
- Laughing over mocktails made with love by Lucky and being moved by Harry's heartfelt love story.

We also ventured into the heart of Bintan on a day tour – cruising through lush mangroves, visiting the Sleeping Buddha, exploring ancient temples, and sharing a seafood feast with a kind father and daughter from Liège, Belgium.

Every moment – big or small – added to the exhilaration of transformation, adventure, and joy.

Empowered Investing: The Journey is the Destination

Every step in life is a chance to connect more deeply – with ourselves, with others, and with what truly matters.

The Bintan *Bond and Beyond Retreat* reminded me that transformation begins within. When we show up with trust and courage, the Universe responds. The women I met there reflected parts of my own path, reminding me that we rise together – through connection, healing, and shared growth.

One truth I now carry: health is our greatest wealth. True vitality means aligning mind, body, and spirit. From this foundation, everything else flows – love, abundance, freedom.

And above all, I realised:

The journey is the destination.

There's no race to the finish. Presence, celebration, and growth are the point.

This retreat deepened my commitment to living a life of purpose, impact, and legacy. A life built through intentional investments in self, family, community, and freedom.

One of the most powerful tools I've used to create that freedom is property investment and development. These assets have helped me build lasting wealth and design a lifestyle I love.

Now, I'm opening the door for other women to do the same – with confidence, clarity, and support. Whether it's your first property, joining a development, or growing a portfolio, you don't have to do it alone.

I'm creating an online course that offers both education and opportunities. You'll learn how to invest, understand the foundations of residential and development projects, and explore real ways to grow wealth while staying aligned with your values.

Under the sea: Life is better down where it's wetter!

An Invitation to Rise

Ready to invest in your future?
Would you love to earn from property development without doing it all yourself?
Curious about becoming a joint venture partner with mentorship and support?

If your answer is 'Yes,' I invite you to **register your interest** in the course or reach out for a conversation about upcoming opportunities.

This is empowered investing – in self, in health, in community, and in legacy.

And this isn't the end – it's just the beginning.

About Carmen Hill

Carmen Hill is an Australian property investor, developer, joint venture partner, NLP-certified mentor, and author of *Empowered Property Investing: Beyond Divorce to Financial Freedom.*

Based in Albury-Wodonga, she's a devoted mum to her son Beau and empowers women to build financial abundance through income-producing assets. A paediatric occupational therapist for 24 years, Carmen blends heart and strategy in her programs.

As a teen, Carmen spent a year on exchange in Canada, igniting her lifelong love for cultural connection. She lives with deep gratitude, valuing contribution, adventure, and raising her son with compassion, purpose, and the courage to fulfill big dreams.

CHAPTER 6 - FELICITY LUCKE
GAINING FREEDOM AND HEALING

*"Before you diagnose yourself with
depression or low self-esteem,
first make sure you are not,
in fact, surrounded by assholes."*
(Sigmund Freud)

Swimming in the ocean at sunrise through a beam of golden sunlight in the calmest of water, which was 29 degrees warm, was nothing short of magical. I will forever treasure this and many other magical moments from Bintan. To say I made the most of this week, to live life to the fullest and experience real pleasure, would be an understatement.

I made so many new connections, tried so many new activities – including aerial yoga, the trapeze, beach parties, limbo, swimming in the ocean at night in my underwear and a midday foam party

– lost two phones temporarily (they decided to stay at Bintan for a bit longer) as well as fulfilling a sexual fantasy and doing many business deals amongst pure indulgence of beach, ocean, nature and a massage or two. Many of these hilarious moments I captured live on the socials, which prompted the question, 'So, you're a travel influencer?'

Life before the retreat felt like navigating a minefield. I was reeling from past childhood traumas, two divorces, including the shadow of a domestic violence marriage, and the inevitable crash of burnout in 2024. My body had finally forced a halt to the relentless hamster wheel of my life as a single mother holding down a job as a people leader as well my coaching business, parenting, trying to 'do' wellness and everyday life stuff ironically mirroring the stress management advice of what to avoid, I'd so often dispensed to others.

I desperately needed space to truly heal from lifelong wounds. This led me to make the very hard decision to leave a corporate job as a people leader in clinical research for a pharmaceutical company – a career that has spanned working for two wonderful companies that have filled my life with many magical experiences and solid lifelong friendships. The company I was leaving had, in fact, supported me by providing emergency accommodation when I was leaving my abusive marriage – something that my local crisis services could not as they had been full since the COVID-19 pandemic.

The *Sydney Entrepreneurs Summit*, a serendipitous *Facebook* find during my first week of my 90-day conscious career break, planted a seed. Maybe I should take my coaching side hustle that I've had since 2019 full-time, after my 90-day career break that I had committed to.

During this event, I met an author who had kindly taken notes for me as I had asked the speaker a question and was standing up with a microphone in my hand. During the next break, we got chatting and I learned she was an author writing on the importance of boundaries. She invited me to a masterclass being held the following week, during which I met Natasa and Stuart Denman.

Witnessing their genuine support for aspiring and first-time authors resonated deeply. When they mentioned the upcoming *Ultimate 48 Hour Author* writers' retreat being held the following week, something inside me just said, 'Yes.'

It felt like the universe was aligning with my need for profound healing and a potential new path through writing. Natasa also mentioned a physical retreat – *Bond and Beyond* – which was to take place on Bintan Island in April 2025. Again, I was a clear yes that came up in me and so I asked to take the last spot. What an amazing decision that would turn out to be.

Before writing my book, *Becoming Bulletproof, from the Brink of Despair to Complete Recovery in 90 Days*, a knot of uncertainty tightened in my stomach frequently. Could I truly let go and be vulnerable with strangers to share my lived experience and subsequent mental health challenges? Would I be able to quiet the noise of my chaotic life long enough to absorb anything meaningful? There were anxieties about the unknown, about stepping so far outside my comfort zone.

While I didn't arrive with rigid expectations, a deep yearning for transformation was definitely present. I hoped for clarity, for a shift in perspective that would help me break free from old patterns. Mostly, I tried to remain open to whatever the experience held, trusting the intuitive pull that had led me there.

A pivotal moment occurred during a conversation with Carmen on the ferry to Bintan. We had just met, yet within the 50-minute ride, we delved into the deepest parts of ourselves. It was a raw, honest exchange, a testament to the immediate sense of safety and connection that permeated the group. We spoke about our past hurts, vulnerabilities, and the hard-won lessons life had etched onto our souls. This conversation set the scene for the conversations yet to come with the other authors and because of the authenticity and realness of these, strong connections were forged quickly amongst a group of people, which on paper may not go together all that way.

Spanning authors from Australia, Canada, the US and the UK, from very different walks of life, lived experiences and ages. Our unwavering empathy and genuine interest in each other's stories created a safe space for vulnerability I hadn't experienced with many people, even those I'd known for years or all my life.

Among all the fun, business strategy and relaxation, we all shared our own experiences with a profound openness that mirrored my own yearning for authentic connection. For so long, I had carried most of the weight of my traumas in isolation, often feeling like a damaged outsider. But here, meeting the fellow authors attending the retreat, I realised I wasn't alone in my struggles. Their vulnerability became a mirror, reflecting my own strength in surviving and a shared human capacity for both pain and resilience.

Furthermore, it confirmed my willingness to be completely seen, flaws and all, and a significant insight struck me.

These weren't just surface-level chats; it was a soul-to-soul recognition. We spoke about the importance of discerning who is a safe space for vulnerability, a lesson many of us had learned through painful experiences. It shifted my perspective on connection. It wasn't about presenting a perfect facade but about finding those rare individuals with whom you can truly be yourself, unfiltered. And this is true for life outside of a retreat.

My biggest lesson here is that you need to be so very careful in who you spend your time with and who you give energy to. Your inner circle is critical for your well-being and support.

In my case, it was an especially hard pill to swallow that some of my closest family members were in fact not in my inner circle – quite to the contrary – on reflection, they have been responsible for the very vast majority of my trauma, abuse and neglect experiences. They had demonstrated that to the finest in the weeks leading up to the retreat, with my epiphany landing on the day I was leaving for the retreat because of their actions on that day.

I realised the joke was on me. I am asking for respect from my loved ones, and yet by keeping certain family members in my inner circle, I was completely disrespecting myself. Frankly, I'd had enough of being taken advantage of and being at the centre of judgement and can do no right by a bunch of highly dysfunctional adults.

Knowing deeply now that, 'It's okay to not be okay, and it's even better when you find someone who understands that without judgment.'

Furthermore, the importance of telling your story and of what it is like to be very authentically you is what attracts the right people into your life. In that moment, a weight lifted. The isolation I had carried for so long began to dissipate. I learned that true connection lies in shared vulnerability and that finding your tribe, even in unexpected places, can be a powerful catalyst for healing. This retreat encounter cracked open a door to a deeper understanding of myself and the profound power of human connection that is based on realness and not some 'perfect' or 'made up' version of us that we thought would keep us safe and or successful.

My connection with the fellow retreat authors, *Club Med* team members and other resort guests was undoubtedly the highlight of the retreat. Throughout the week, we gravitated towards each other, sharing meals, reflections, and laughter.

This relationship taught me the profound impact of being truly seen and heard without judgement. I believe it helps us to soften the edges we develop as a defence mechanism to past hurt. It was a reminder that connection isn't about shared history but about a shared understanding of the human experience and how each of us has walked a unique path that can still bind us in some way, if we are willing to share our story and perspectives, as well as stay open when it differs to that of others around us.

There was a specific evening, sitting under the starlit Bintan sky, sharing stories and quiet companionship with Carmen and a few other women, where I felt an undeniable sense of belonging. It wasn't just about shared experiences at the retreat; it was a feeling of being part of a collective consciousness, a group of individuals on their own healing journeys, supporting and uplifting each other.

In that moment, the isolation I had often felt melted away, replaced by a powerful sense of community and shared humanity.

Some of the unforgettable moments include the dancing evenings after dinner. These inevitably turned into full-blown, joyous expressions of freedom. There was no self-consciousness, no judgement, just a collective letting go. I found myself laughing uncontrollably as I attempted some questionable dance moves alongside women I had only just met, yet felt a deep kinship with.

The air crackled with pure, unadulterated joy. We were all just present in that moment, lost in the rhythm and the shared laughter. It was a reminder of the simple, childlike pleasure of movement and music, something I had perhaps forgotten in the seriousness of my healing journey.

This moment taught me the vital importance of embracing play and spontaneity as well as your intuition. It wasn't about achieving anything or analysing the experience; it was simply about being present, listening to your inner knowing that we all have and allowing joy to bubble up. It highlighted how laughter and shared fun can be incredibly therapeutic, a powerful antidote to stress and worry. It was a beautiful reminder that even amidst deep strategic business work, personal growth and healing, there is always room for light-heartedness and the pure, uninhibited enjoyment and pleasure of life.

I am undeniably different now compared to when I arrived. The weight of isolation has lessened, replaced by a newfound sense of connection, self-love and acceptance of what is around me that is beyond my control. The retreat acted as a catalyst, accelerating my healing process in ways I hadn't anticipated. I feel lighter, more grounded, and more attuned to my own needs.

I am taking with me a profound understanding of the power of vulnerability and authentic connection. The bonds forged, particularly with Carmen and Luba, have shown me the importance of finding my tribe and allowing myself to be truly seen. I also carry the memory of shared joy and the reminder to embrace spontaneity and playfulness in my daily life. The lessons learned about setting boundaries and prioritising self-care have been deeply reinforced.

Moving forward, I will actively cultivate the connections I made at the retreat. I intend to be more open and vulnerable in my relationships, fostering deeper and more authentic bonds. Professionally, this experience has solidified my desire to share my story through writing, running my own retreats and coaching, helping others navigate their own healing journeys. The enforced pause of my career break, despite its unexpected twists, has clarified my path.

I am committed to prioritising self-care without guilt, recognising it not as a luxury but as a necessity. The spontaneous joy experienced during the retreat has inspired me to incorporate more fun and play into my routine. My outlook has shifted from one of isolated struggle to one of hopeful connection and resilient self-awareness. My plans now include actively building a supportive community and continuing to explore the power of shared experiences in healing and growth.

The retreat was not an endpoint but rather a significant turning point, setting me on a more authentic and joyful trajectory.

If you are on the fence about saying 'Yes' to an experience like this, I would wholeheartedly encourage you to take the leap. It's in stepping outside your comfort zone that the most profound growth often occurs. Trust the intuitive pull that might be whispering to you, even if fear or doubt tries to hold you back.

My biggest piece of advice for embracing personal growth, connection, or transformation is to be open and vulnerable. Allow yourself to be seen, even the parts you might feel are broken or imperfect. It is in this vulnerability that true connection is forged and healing begins. Embrace the unknown, trust the process, and know that you are not alone on your journey.

Saying yes to yourself and to experiences that call to your soul can be the most courageous and rewarding decision you ever make.

Be brave, be open, and allow the possibility of profound transformation to unfold.

Felicity, Nat and Luba chatting and floating in the ocean.

Dancing away at the foam party in Bintan.

Nat and Felicity at the White Party.

About Felicity Lucke

Felicity Lucke is an author, speaker and advocate for those affected by abuse, neurodiversity and mental health challenges. Through her 17 years of corporate leadership, six years of business ownership as well as lived experience, she has helped over 7,000 people find their voice, experience self-love and find the will to live a life with joy and gratitude after personal setbacks, leadership challenges, burnout and trauma.

These teachings were achieved through her books, workshops, coaching, speaking engagements and retreats, as well as business ventures creating opportunities for wellness, pleasure and financial independence.

Today, Felicity lives on the stunning northern beaches of Sydney with her two children and two Italian greyhound puppies.

Felicity is available for strategic partnerships, investments, consultancy and speaking engagements, as well as workshops and retreats.

Connect with Felicity via her website or on her socials.

Felicity Lucke

felicity@felicitylilylucke.com
www.felicitylilylucke.com

CHAPTER 7 - CLAIRE WHITE

FROM BURNOUT TO CRYSTAL-CLAIRE BRILLIANCE

*"If it is to be
It's up to me!"*
(William H. Johnsen)

On arrival at *Club Med Bintan*, 18 excited women witnessed the sunlit palms at balcony height in the main reception area. This vista just blew me away. Standing at frond level was lovely. I felt at one with the earth, sky, and sea.

The ocean's aqua marine shades stretching to the horizon were simply breathtaking. A few scattered fluffs of cloud contrasted with the blue sky. The massive white beach extending off the lush grass and the swimming pools beckoned. I took photos and knew I'd soon be in that water.

A rush came with the immediate knowing that we were in for something totally awesome. Wow factor. YES.

As a nurse, recognising burnout and the need for self-care overtook staying home to complete my second book, *Aye-Aye Captain*, with its exciting dine-out stories of our 30 years at sea despite Parkinson's Disease. I'd booked this retreat many months ago, enjoying the anticipation, yet some of the preparations were nightmarish, because again, there was no respite care available until so close to departure. The stress was palpable. I'd been in tears searching for help.

Conspiring against my epiphany from the time of his brain surgery, that looking after Number 1 (me) was imperative to look after anyone else, my husband Errol's Parkinsons Disease deterioration made him fall nearly every day, sometimes more than once. It was distressing. My health was also out of balance. Disturbed sleep from active and vocal dreams, night time assistance mobilising, and helicopter-type vigilance wore me out. Knowing I couldn't sustain his 24/7 care alone, had my arm raised for help to avoid crashing.

A fall caused a nasty head gash the day before he was booked in for 'pain management' of his shoulders, covering respite care. Further treatment, checks, and admission in case of brain bleeding were necessary. Fortunately, all was clear, so off I flew. It's awful leaving when a loved one is hospitalised, yet I knew he was in good hands.

Knowing others, like me, are seeking happiness despite difficult times, allowed me to step back into my power, celebrating my first book, *Who's In charge, My Brain or Me... (or My Wife) Navigating Life With Parkinson's* was such an achievement, I felt the lessons learned really primed me for my second book. This retreat was about rediscovering myself.

We all seek to fulfil needs and learn about life. It became crystal-clear that I needed to 'don my own oxygen mask' first, as they say. Others may take it, even on a retreat. A pause, deep breath, mental reset, and honouring personal boundaries are keys to our wellness. This retreat was just 'what the doctor ordered' and better than the brochures. I was open to whatever unfolded. It was deserved and so appreciated. I had insurance, so I knew I could fly home to Errol for some emergency.

The group understood my need for a break, recognising we are a couple normally joined at the hip, and they saw me totally relax and tune into holiday mode. Being with widows, and some separated women, also gave me greater appreciation for still having a loving life partner in a world where connection is sometimes craved. I'm super grateful for the friendships made through sharing this entire experience. I know it has changed my life, and I can hardly wait for the rendezvous at the next one.

Overcoming insane fear by taking the leap of faith on a high-flying trapeze (despite safety nets and harnesses) allowed me to shift this fear into fun and bliss. The intensity, adrenaline, and pure fear were real, even if slightly surprising given my history of participating in extreme sports. I'm even overcoming the well-recognised world number one fear of public speaking!

Knowing I am ultimately in charge of this one great life opportunity, eases my connections with like-minded others who understand the ultimate joy of achievement. It empowers me to believe that I can do what I set my mind to.

Relaxing on Bintan Island, in the beautiful tropical Riau group of Indonesia, was only a 45-minute fast ferry ride from Singapore. I embraced being back in Southeast Asia, where we'd previously cruised aboard our own boats, *'Idlewise'* then *'Restless M'*, for over a decade. I felt downright lucky to have already sailed from nearby Bantam Island to Bintan on the historic ketch Rona (Circa 1895).

Knowledge of the local language brought more understanding and smiles. We each relax into holiday mode in our own way.

For some, its floating in the sea, dancing until dawn, trying lots of different cocktails and foods, joining in the water and sporting activities, moon, star, cloud and general nature gazing, sun-baking, having massages, quiet moments of reflection, special rituals, trying different perspectives – aerial yoga, headstands or cartwheels, gathering washed-in flotsam, pondering how to clean up the world, sending out love and healing through prayer, making new connections, meeting others from around the globe, reconnection with those at home, having meaningful discussions, reading, sleeping, sharing our deepest most personal joys and our concerns, or quietly finding a moment of peace for ourselves with music, meditation, or laughter.

Saying 'YES' sometimes means saying 'NO' to other repetitive distractions. I've learned that with age comes the wisdom to see what is personally good for us and what needs to be let go. There were times for listening and times to say enough listening when the woes of others and the world began sucking the oxygen right from my face.

Children sometimes don't realise how loud their squeals can be, sometimes joyful, sometimes not, and I met adults who also didn't have a regulator. We don't know what we don't know. There were brave and adventurous souls everywhere, all with stories to share. Some were so utterly inspirational, I listened for hours; some were still in tough places, and some leaned on the bar more than others. It's a small world, after all... By simply chatting about accents, it became apparent that my newest South

African friends met at the spa, also knew another countryman and relative; John Matambo. RIP.

All these, and so much more, at Bintan took me to my own Zen bliss. I exercised respecting my boundaries and even excused myself a few times. The scenery was spectacular, with *Bond and Beyond* success anchoring deep into my heart. A physical and emotional memory anchor is in my wristband, the *Club Med* room entry key, which somehow fortunately missed being cut off. It takes me to some of the most beautiful memories possible.

The pivoting transformation continues to ripple out for me every day through bonds of friendship; ideas, encouragement, business learning, aspirations, dreams, and anticipation of another no doubt life-changing retreat next year. I'm in! Take my money!

New friendships formed for me with our entire group... While at the beach, the sea, dance floors, around the pool and bars, dining, and sharing fabulous activities, even at the spa massage experience. Speaking Indonesian and some Arabic impressed staff who were already incredibly friendly. I'm sure this paved the way for being invited to a local Muslim wedding.

I was privileged enough to bring Carmen, a retreat friend, knowing this experience would be amazing for her, too. We caught a taxi at night to Rekoh village, met *Club Med* cook Ian's family, and then Hendry, the groom. His Australian bride, Teagan, had little local language. Hendry was so happy having us there for her. I felt we were a strong connection to Australia (home) at this very special time. Truly, we felt honoured being in her changing room, talking girl-talk. Also, having foreigners at an Indonesian wedding is considered good luck.

Claire and Carmen attending the Indonesian wedding.

I also felt part of something bigger when stirring the Beef Rendang curry over the open fire in preparation for the next day's feast and leading all the children to sing their national anthem with me. The words returned, surprising me too! Even though these weren't part of retreat activities, it reinforced how exciting life can be when we seize the moment and take opportunities.

ANZAC Day 2025 we commemorated 110 years since the Gallipoli landing. Being in a foreign land and on the beach at dawn was deeply moving for me as I thanked those who gave the ultimate price of life for our freedom. We will remember them.

For me, our retreat motto of *Bond and Beyond* was fulfilled in such unexpected ways as these.

The unforgettable moments within our retreat group were numerous. Standout personal growth came from classroom shares, as we crazy danced with wild abandon to our fast beat theme song and laughed at some of the things said that you have to be there for to understand properly.

My touch and smell book cover idea became 'Scratch and Sniff' and somehow took off on a hilariously different tangent when rallied around the room.

The first aha! moment from our group classroom that resonated for me was: Do not take feedback, nor even take so-called 'constructive criticism' from those who don't have the results you want. Remain open, but don't take criticism from someone you wouldn't go to for advice. The old question, 'Would you mind if I gave you some feedback?' can make us gag.

'Seek first to understand' is so important. Otherwise, it means, 'Would you mind if I gave you some negative feedback from my perspective, disguised as constructive criticism, whether or not you want or need it?'

Fantastic, though, was the child-like fun time enjoyed in the foam-bubble party. It was a first for me and I played out fully! There's something special about unbridled fun! I'm ever so grateful to my playmates. I haven't needed lessons in having fun in life, as I'm easily socially excited, yet as a 64-year-old with a couple of extra kilos bonded to my bones, I jiggled off lots of calories without even knowing, as it was exercise disguised as fun; Therein lies another epiphany for me. Each of us brought some advice:

Smash it out!
Love God!
Dreams come true!

Be you!
Just imagine!
Be it! Be about it!
Courage. Speak out!
Master your mojo!
Make beautiful choices!
Get shit done!
You've got this babe!
Stay inspired!
You can do it!

> "Great people have one thing in common –
> they lack conformity."
> (PK Shaw)

I embrace this wholeheartedly, except when in Rome! Don't worry, be happy! I've learned that worrying about what is beyond our control is pointless, as it changes nothing and, in the end, makes us feel miserable. Worry also makes us spiritually unfruitful. Happiness is contagious! The main message I love to share is this powerful sentence of 10 two-letter words:

IF IT IS TO BE, IT IS UP TO ME.

Some of the group gems shared were: Ask for help. Take safe risks. Declutter. It's OK to be great! Blessed. Grateful. Abundant. Be creative. Seek clarity. Value plan. Step into your power. Action kills procrastination. The harder I work, the luckier I get. Never cancel an event. Create value. Give bang for your buck. Luck is where preparation and opportunity meet; anything else is pure chance. Success leaves clues. Schedule it. Power is proximity. Surround yourself with like-minded people. Value is a feeling, not a calculation. Remain solution-focused. Be yourself. Authenticity sells. Keep being yourself. The more fun you have, the more money you make. Follow what you love.

Remember your 'Why'/Purpose/Drive. Do the hardest thing first (eat the frog). Coherence creates resonance (understanding), so ensure your clients see you practising that. Follow up, follow up, follow up. Data-based decisions. Speed to lead – aka speed of implementation. Social media can be fun. Use *ChatGPT*. Love the game of business.

I know I am making a difference in the world, raising awareness and funds for Parkinson's research and a cure, in selling my book, just as every drop in the ocean amounts to a lot. I serve others by giving back with hope for a world free of P.D. It gives me a new focus on something big in the world. Upselling my expertise also benefits others, especially those affected by P.D. or in a carer's role. I'm taking home renewed confidence and increased awareness of avoiding carer stress.

My priority is quality time with Errol, and I'm so grateful for the chapter in my life at Bintan Island that took me 'From Burnout to Brilliance'. Now there's a title!

I know possibilities are endless and that I can do anything when empowered. I already know that enthusiasm is the mother of success. I'm feeling the love and support from all my sisters on this *Bond and Beyond Retreat* and am leaning forward, as they say in the bush, to next year's retreat in beautiful Bali. The possibilities between now and then are bountiful.

The world is so beautiful when our hearts are full of love, and mine is bursting to the brim. My cup is also full, and I've learned to allow others to only drink from the saucer. This way, there is no depletion from my full cup, and I am grateful for opportunities that come my way, even those brilliantly disguised as impossible situations! I promise to also take good care of myself! Do yourself a favour and come, too.

If you're hesitating on the edge about taking the jump to book in, DON'T.

Just do it now! I hesitated last year, and it was fully booked, so when a space became available, I trusted the process, jumped in, and the magic happened.

New experiences can be daunting, and it's often in the vulnerable moments that we discover our true potential. You will thank yourself for overcoming fear and excuses. The profound power of connection and learning about myself and others through fun has really sunk into my bones on this *Bond and Beyond Retreat*.

We have laughed and cried together, reminding me we're never alone on our journeys. It's with so much love and gratitude to Natasa, Vivienne, Julie, Wendy, and all *Bond and Beyonders* (including courtesy Aunties and me) that I add my biggest piece of advice...

Allow yourself to be vulnerable and uncomfortable, because it's through embracing challenges that we grow and transform. Experiences that fire our spirit, inspiring change, often seem just beyond reach.

Join us next year.

You will love yourself for it!

Claire leading the dance charge in the training room.

Nat and Claire at the White Night.

About Claire White

Claire White is a specialist nurse, sailor, public speaker, and author of *Who's In Charge, My Brain Or Me? (Or My Wife...) Navigating Life With Parkinson's*.

She was first mate of the 180 T mini ship for almost 30 years and is married to Captain Errol, who was formally diagnosed with Parkinson's Disease in 2002.

Claire is dedicated to raising awareness and funds for Parkinson's research and a cure. Her personal story of adventurous navigating aboard inspires others to better understand the concerns of individuals with any dis-ease.

Despite facing a reverse sea- change becoming land-based, Claire remains dedicated, enthusiastic, and passionate about making a global difference starting at home.

CHAPTER 8 - CHRISTINE JUDD

THE POWER OF SHOWING UP

*"The willingness to show up changes us,
it makes us a little braver each time."*
(Brene Brown)

Walking through the halls of Sydney International Airport, a myriad of memories came flooding through me from countless trips before, and from countless airports, particularly during my 13 years living abroad. It seemed like a lifetime ago, yet, the excitement of travelling, the throng of fellow travellers in all states of organisation and chaos, were my company as I waited for my flight to board.

Once upon a time, I had indeed lived the gypsy life. Based in a meditation centre in India, I would return to Australian home shores at least once a year for a month or so, never putting down roots, visiting, and then take off again to beloved India. My travel plans often threw in a 'turnaround' as we called it, to another location on the globe that took my fancy.

A 'turnaround' in essence occurred when my Indian tourist visa had run out and I needed to go out of the country to get a new one in order to come back into India. These turnaround locations included Italy, the south of France and Paris, Munich, Berlin and Luxemburg, San Francisco and Bangkok. The world had been my oyster as I worked ways to reach all kinds of places where I had formed new friends and was invited, from connections made in India at the meditation centre.

We were all savvy travellers back then and travelling by necessity included a kind of hustle in how we worked tickets, airlines, itineraries, visas and making our dollars go that extra mile.

Now as I sat within the bustling halls of Terminal 1, I had actually not stepped onto an international flight since before the COVID-19 pandemic – a trip to Hawaii for my 50th birthday (my own personal *Hawaii Five-Oh*!). It was now, six years later, that the adventurer in me – the part that needed something new, something expansive and exotic and well frankly, unknown – had stepped forward once more.

As I looked for somewhere to sit myself on this autumn afternoon, I was kind of stressed, I was a little melancholic, I was nervous and grouchy, yet simultaneously, I was excited and deeply optimistic, as I took freedom in my hands and stepped away from the comfort of my usual life.

The Promise of Adventure

I immediately recognised the opportunity to be had through this trip, and how much I could benefit from the experience right now. Over the last decade, I had prioritised other parts of my life such as my work and financial security as key areas of attention and activity, and had made great inroads. I was working roles that combined trauma work with complexity of circumstances and social factors; my reputation as a mental health social worker and therapist were reaching an incredibly fulfilling, mature place. I managed to advocate for myself over and over to work with the clients that I felt were my forte: trauma recovery with drug and alcohol work and enduring mental health conditions.

However, despite the great fulfilment I also felt an increasing loss of vitality and overall movement in myself. I missed a certain 'get up and go', energy to meet life and all the intensities it brought to me. This kind of lag in me seemed to come into form and be amplified by the COVID-19 pandemic and long lockdowns. I knew now that I certainly had the capacity to put down roots and stay the course; the readiness for more dynamic movement and vitality beckoned.

From various stages across my life, I knew the amazing value to be had in shaking things up by choosing differently, experimenting, and stepping away from familiar everyday routines in order to get clarity, insight and freshness in my life. I knew the value of stepping out of the familiar through a good holiday. I knew how a 'good holiday' can be so elusive. And I knew why...

Bonding and Beyond...

The *Ultimate Retreat* definitely promised to reconnect me with my gypsy, travelling self of long ago. I hoped to restore or perhaps re-align that part of myself through the movement and dynamism of our retreat together. I missed spreading my wings, travelling lightly, the adventure and richness of cultural diversity, and the benefit of getting away from the routine and mundane, to see things within myself and my world more clearly.

Distance offers a wonderful opportunity to gain fresh and sometimes new perspectives on all aspects of the world and ourselves in it... This is real social worker territory! It involved a trip overseas to another vastly different culture with a group of similar-minded people: we had all written books and worked with our publisher; we had all signed up for this particular experience. Common ground, common ground, common ground.

The invitation to travel with a group of authors, warmly facilitated and organised through my publishing company, had seemed too good to resist. The invitation had come with a strong dose of enthusiasm, speaking of a wonderful balance of fun, focus, and replenishment through the holiday together.

Firstly, what can I say but it appealed to the part of me ready to have a proper holiday! What could be more basic and essential, yet it was the fundamental truth. I wanted a break and had taken time off in the past without necessarily shifting my energy levels and headspace to a fresh, restored level. I wanted something different and new, knowing that it was this that could help me genuinely reset. The idea of prioritising times of retreat, a break from routine living and all the mundane stuff of everyday life, immediately spoke to me without much requirement to think.

BUT it also appealed to me because of the social limitations I felt within myself, and simultaneously, the wish to be more comfortable in larger groups, parties even, and an overall longing to connect. I have always best related one-to-one, versus a big group. I have always had a few, deep friendships, and my work is about being in the depths in therapeutic conversations with singular clients routinely. I was like a fish out of water in bigger groups with a lot of talking, often left feeling drained. So, I came for *Bonding and Beyonding*... A play with being in the bigger group of people.

For these reasons, this chapter could have been called 'Travelling and holidaying with others when you are an introvert', 'Celebrating connection with a group of strangers when you have had interpersonal wounding', or 'Stepping into the nightmare of a large group of people because the emotional part of you longs to be more comfortable around people' (okay, this last one may be me being deliberately dramatic).

In the invitation to this retreat, I also saw an opportunity to be challenged and to enjoy, to trust myself and genuinely engage. I wanted to test my own capacity to find and respect my limits, and how I might expand them. I wanted to find my way beyond this lifelong limitation.

I knew that the people included in this offer of a retreat were from a dynamic community, a group of unique individuals, of people engaged in life.

From my experiences at various events, we were all fellow authors and, as authors, were creative and had stories to tell. These dynamic qualities often emerged from being creative (but not necessarily so for all, many might not identify as creative), having a sense of purpose in life, and frequently living a life 'outside the box'.

Although I did not know anyone else going, I trusted the leadership and I also trusted that the organisation of the trip would be of a high quality. This was my opportunity!

A key tip for doing your own retreat:

Know what you hope for from the trip, and the 'growth edge' that this trip brings renewed possibility to.

My Tool for Exploration

As a meditator for many years daily, I had discovered that being present to yourself – as you are in meditation or mindfulness practice – is a simple yet potent practice for the following reasons:

- It offers a holistic and complete sense of yourself
- The sense of yourself includes the body and senses, a 'felt sense' of self, helpful for people with anxiety or trauma
- The practice of meditation (being present in the here and now with everything that is present, without judgment, allowing everything to be as it is observed) is built on non-judgemental, unconditional witnessing or what simply is, so it can remove self-judgement and loss of connection with self
- Being present is actually 'showing up' in the social sense to both inner and outer realities in an effective, neat practice.

Thus, besides a holiday with my publisher to a beautiful destination, the retreat and break offered me a chance of practicing showing up and staying true to myself wanting to be a part of it.

What is Showing Up?

*"Give yourself permission to allow this moment
to be exactly as it is, and allow yourself
to be exactly as you are."*
(Jon Kabat-Zinn)

From many years of practising meditation, I have progressively showed up more in my life. Showing up means actually bringing my whole self to something, or, in an absolutely real way, bringing as much as I can of me when I am 'on', showing up to meet others and spending time together in as whole a state as possible. Showing up means I bring my whole self to the present moment.

I can find two key elements of showing up which include:

- Consciously being open to the world around me in this moment, including with people.
- Owning and taking responsibility for who I am each moment, including feeling my strengths and where I flow in connection, and simultaneously, owning the parts of me that may be tainted with lack of confidence, ease or vitality. It includes a part of me that has actively avoided others in service of finding people difficult and for my own self-preservation, feeling my sense of self as fragile and elusive.

I took these with me to Bintan and they became my supports for connection and social joy.

A Path of Meditation

*"To begin to meditate is to look into our
lives with interest, in kindness and discover
how to be wakeful and free."*
(Jack Kornfield)

Meditation or mindfulness practice is the practice of being present, open, and accessible in and to the present moment. Through meditation my outcomes were the following:

- It is indeed a practice; there is no right or wrong, success or failure, good or bad. Phew! Thankfully, there just is practice.
- Meditation or mindfulness is energy work on oneself of the highest quality: dealing only with what is, offering no judgement, no agenda, no effort; a continual happening that unfolds.
- Meditation or mindfulness practice combined with a break away in a beautiful location, among a group of diverse and mature people, offers a restorative and fertile retreat. With space from the daily life, insights, important recognitions, relaxation and space, pleasure, connection and discovery, all are able to emerge. Their value is beyond measure and the benefits offered can be carried back into our everyday life.
- Feeling your feet on the ground encourages a felt sense of yourself that includes your physical body.
- The body is always present through tuning into the five senses and beyond, the body is an anchor and resource, the body literally hosts our life, is the site of emotions and expression, of esteem and self-care and respect. It has much information and communication to offer us in showing up in our physicality.
- Long ago I learned that wherever you go, there you are. Moving location cannot address discomfort within oneself, ultimately. It takes effort and energy to censor oneself and keep disowned parts and their associated needs at bay.
- 'Paradise found' is an inner state. I know it to be true, yet, so often in my life such a reckoning and realisation

ebbs and flows. Sometimes I am grounded in this knowing and at other times it eludes me, as I inhabit a place of not knowing, discomfort and the need to keep going despite a lack of clarity.
- Look for an opportunity to travel and/or retreat with a group of other people where there is a common purpose, interest or project that has linked you up (this helps to logically know that the tour is safe, grounded, well-planned and there are pre-existing common threads with fellow travellers).
- A key lesson from this experience is that showing up allows re-engaging with being active and shaping my life.

Conversations to be Had, Partnerships to be Forged

The group of fellow travellers consisted of a broad variety of characters, from varying backgrounds and of different talents. I was deeply impressed by all of the women who were writing books or had already written books for a larger purpose, and the journeys that they had been on. In my quest for rich contact, I had hit the jackpot, spotting wonderful values and skills in colourful action. I listened a lot, and it was wonderful listening.

One of the deepest conversations I had however occurred on the very first morning as myself and Sydney, an artist and healer from Sedona, Arizona, went through immigration at the Singapore Ferry Terminal. It was the first day of our retreat together and literally our first meeting. Our conversation seemed to gather a wonderful fire beneath it and continued across our pile of luggage and along gangways and wobbling planks, as we boarded the ferry to the island of Bintan, Indonesia.

The trip sped by as we talked and asked questions; our conversation was one of mutual understanding of hard things, of recovery and the way that each of our creative practices had played such a key, central role in overcoming and maintaining our personal healing. We had different words and language for things, we had had different ways of keeping our creativity going at different stages of our life, yet there was something shared on a deep level that was our common ground.

It was the beginning of an important connection for me.

On this journey as we were getting to know each other, I had speculated lightly to Sydney about my third book. I sensed an opportunity as we sat, sailing across a silvery flat strait in the ferry. 'Oh, I actually have thought about writing a book on creativity.'

It was great to say it to a fellow creative, one who also lived a similarly spiritual life.

Our friendship continued during the retreat gently, but the moment that marked the peak, came the next morning as we woke up on beautiful, tropical Bintan.

I had arrived at breakfast and I sat down. Opposite me, Sydney sat and immediately asked if I wanted to collaborate on the book on creativity. I said 'Yes', it was a wonderful, promising offer. It came out of the blue; I was really surprised and still am. But it summed up the possibility of partnership and innovation, that can come from meeting new people in fresh environments, and clicking with someone beyond words, in a similar business of life.

I recognised that I would be able to develop my own creativity, my own work with people in a deep way, AND I could do this with a collaborator and sharer of the journey. Bingo! It was day one and however I was showing up seemed pretty good to me.

NB: If you are interested in the outcome of our partnership and if creativity is on your exploration list, please look for our book!

The Last Message

Taking a retreat for restoration, and to harness innovation and creativity is highly recommended to all.

Showing up as fully as possible for enjoyment, a break or retreat, in the company of others in all their splendid diversity, is ultimately showing up for yourself, honouring what you need and who you are, in an alert, aware and robust way.

It is the best.

On the mangrove tour with Vivi, Julie and Zoe.

Christine and Sydney in Little India.

Enjoying the retreat with Claire and Felicity.

About Christine Judd

Christine Judd is a qualified counsellor, psychotherapist and mental health social worker. She has experience working in women's health, with trauma, problem gambling and addictions, mental illness, family violence, and personality disorders. She currently works in a service supporting people with mental health issues alongside drug and alcohol concerns. She also works in private practice as a clinical supervisor.

Chris is author of *Beyond Stormy Weather: Keys to Understanding, Navigating and Embracing your Emotions*, and is publishing a second book this year titled *The Little Book of Trauma Recovery: 99 Everyday Tips and Tools for Authentic Healing*.

Both are available through her website *christinejudd.com.au* or at your local book outlet.

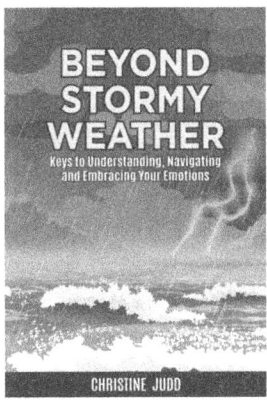

Christine lives in the Orange region of NSW, Australia, with her cat and dogs, plays violin, trumpet, and enjoys long walks in nature. She is passionate about advocating for better emotional health for all, the power of creativity, and the richness of a life truly lived.

CHAPTER 9 - SYDNEY FRANCIS
BEYOND METAMORPHOSIS

"Some of us have made an idol out of exhaustion. The only time we know we have done enough is when we are running on empty and when the ones we love the most are the ones we see the least... I began to wonder if my human wholeness might be more useful to God than my exhausting goodness."
(Barbara Brown Taylor)

I felt a bit queasy. I had just slammed my first Singapore coffee at the café in the ferry terminal – hot, thick, syrupy-sweet with condensed milk (yummy!) – and it was now sloshing uneasily in my stomach. As I boarded the ferry, the air was dense, slightly metallic, with that sterile chill of over-conditioned spaces that have held too many bodies for too long. I could feel the familiar swirl of nervous energy pulsing just under my skin.

I looked for a seat with the group and I noticed how low the ceilings were, how tightly the rows of seats were packed together. The air in the cabin smelled heavy of damp salt and engine oil. I squeezed into my seat, brushing shoulders with the other authors in my group. My body, still recalibrating from time zone shifts and airport fatigue, was on edge.

Then the engines fired up – first a deep rumble, then a steady growl that vibrated through the soles of my feet. We lurched away from the dock, leaving the city behind. Through the foggy windows, the harbour blurred into grey-green water and mist. The motion of the boat rocked my body in a way that both unsettled and soothed me.

I struck up a conversation with the author sitting next to me, Christine Judd. I didn't know it yet, but this trip wasn't just a crossing of water – it was a crossing into something far deeper. The ferry shuddered forward, and I was on my way not just to Bintan Island, but toward an awakening I hadn't yet named.

What began as queasiness and noise quietly gave way to something else: resonance.

And unknowingly, I was just about to embark on an epic friendship.

There are moments in life when a quiet truth lands inside you so clearly, it shakes the walls of everything you thought you knew. For me, that moment happened at the *2025 Bond and Beyond Retreat*, when I suddenly realised I had been depressed for the past several months. Not tired. Not just uninspired. Depressed. And I hadn't seen it.

Before the retreat, I had been dragging myself through the days, utterly depleted, both physically and emotionally. I'd just closed my bricks-and-mortar business that never quite clicked, no matter how hard I pushed over the past year. I had also been very sick with stage four GERD; so for months, I cancelled clients and coasted on fumes.

I wasn't creating. I wasn't dreaming. I was just surviving.

That's the thing about depression – sometimes, you don't even recognise it until you step into a different rhythm. Until you hear someone like Natasa Denman speak passionately about loving the game of business, and you realise something is off.

During the second session with Nat, *Beyond Business*, I felt the jolt of the a-ha moment. Nat was talking about loving the game of business. And I just couldn't resonate with it.

At first, I concluded that I don't love business and maybe I should rethink what I have been doing with my life. But as I continued the trip, spent more time with the other authors, gathered more energy, and then returned home to integrate and process my experience, it dawned on me that it isn't about the business at all.

I have been in a depression for the past several months, and I haven't had the energy, excitement, or passion to take pleasure in anything, much less my business.

I came home from the retreat with more than jet lag and a suitcase full of Southeast Asian treasures. I came home with self-awareness.

On Wednesday, after unpacking, sharing said treasures with my family, and snuggling my pets, I went to the doctor for a thyroid check-up. My levels were off after 10 or more years of being at the same dosage. More importantly, I shared honestly about how I'd been feeling – the fatigue, the hopelessness, the disinterest in everything I once enjoyed. She looked at me with softness and concern and gently suggested I consider antidepressants, as well as counselling.

At first, the suggestion rattled me. Was I really that bad off? But almost immediately, I felt something else: relief. A sense of confirmation. I wasn't lazy. I wasn't broken. I was depressed. And now I could start doing something about it.

For most of my life, I've danced with both anxiety and depression. I just didn't always know that's what it was. I grew up walking on eggshells, attempting to stay invisible, trying to please a narcissistic mother.

When my father died when I was 10, it cemented the feeling that love and security were precarious, fragile things. I learned to stay small, to scan for danger, to overperform. I shaped my life around making others comfortable. That's the origin of the saviour complex I carried for years.

But this retreat showed me that I no longer need to be anyone's saviour. Not even my own.

Letting go of that role is disorienting. If I'm not the fixer, the healer, the one who holds it all together for everyone else — who am I? That question lives at the centre of my current transformation. It's not just about recovering from depression. It's about rebuilding my identity. It's about dissolving everything that isn't me, so that I can become more of me.

And that's where the black butterfly comes in.

Butterflies, both literal and symbolic, were everywhere on this trip. I saw several flying around the beautiful gardens of the resort. Then, fellow author Zoe MacBean shared that she saw a black butterfly. In the past, she felt that the metaphor of the butterfly was, perhaps, overused and cliché. Yet, she researched the black butterfly and discovered that its message was meaningful to her.

Later, I shared my Spirit Oracle cards with the group and Nat received the 'Butterfly Spirit' card. To me, that seemed so perfect for Nat, who is like a Butterfly Guardian Spirit, guiding soon-to-be authors with their personal transformation journeys of writing and publishing their books.

Several times throughout the trip, I saw these mysterious black butterflies and noted them in my journal. I also saw a black dragonfly and a snake that was copper and black with teal spots. The repeated incidence of butterflies stimulated a reflective process about which stage of the butterfly's life cycle I was in: egg, caterpillar, chrysalis, or butterfly.

Each stage has a unique meaning and set of actions to support that part of the process. It struck me that I was likely in the chrysalis phase, and that my recent depression was related to letting go of my old identity as a healer, constructed around pleasing others so that I could stay safe.

I also found the colour black meaningful. At home, in Sedona, Arizona, I have not seen any black butterflies; we have swallowtails, monarchs, and other white, orange, and yellow butterflies, but not fully black.

According to Ted Andrews, author of *Animal Speak*, black signifies protection, birth, magic, secretiveness, and sacrifice. In other sources on animal symbolism, black symbolises the void, the formless, and the dreamtime – a liminal state of all possibility and unrealised potential, a state between death and rebirth.

I see the perfect metaphor in the butterfly's metamorphosis. In order to become a butterfly, the caterpillar doesn't grow wings. It melts.

Inside the chrysalis, it becomes a kind of cellular soup. There is no identity. No form. Just dissolution. And in that surrender, a new creature is born.

That's where I am. In the chrysalis. In the goo.

And let me tell you, it is not graceful. As a self-conscious being, I find it painful to let go of the old forms and patterns and enter a transitional state of not knowing. My ego is built around my past experiences and is comforted by believing, 'I know,' and therefore, I am in control. Most days, I wake up with an intense fear of uncertainty, which I choose to overcome with trust in God and a faith in a larger process unfolding.

During this process, I've slept more than I think I should. I missed events I would normally enjoy. I skipped adventures like the mangrove boat tour or the trapeze, even though a part of me wants to say 'Yes'. Even snorkelling, which I usually love, took a hit. I didn't feel like myself. But maybe that's the point. I'm not myself. I'm becoming something new.

The beauty is, I wasn't alone.

On the ferry to Bintan, I sat next to Christine, and within minutes, we clicked. We shared stories about art, healing, and emotional transformation. She told me she was completing a book on trauma healing and had another in the pipeline about creativity. I had an immediate intuitive hit: ask to collaborate. I barely knew her, but by the time we docked, I was dreaming of co-writing a book on creativity with Chris.

That connection was an immediate soul recognition. Our time together on the beach later that week, brainstorming ideas and sketching out concepts, was a balm to my spirit. I remembered who I was. A creator. A visionary. An alchemist.

And that is what depression had stolen from me: **My creativity.**

Creativity is the opposite of depression. It is life force. It is breath. When I'm creating, I feel connected to myself, to Spirit, to purpose. When I'm not, I feel like a ghost inside my own life.

Since the *Bond and Beyond Retreat*, I've been exploring what it means to come back to that spark. To move through my mental health challenges with compassion. To accept the possibility that maybe I've had bipolar type II all along, with hypomanic bursts of productivity and long valleys of exhaustion and depression. I've started researching. I've talked to my doctor. I'm not looking for a label – I'm looking for understanding.

Because when I understand myself, I can care for myself.

And when I care for myself, I can create.

This chapter of my life is not about doing more. It's about doing differently. It's about designing a life that honours my cycles, my needs, my truth. It's about shedding the structures that were built to please others and stepping into my own authority.

It's about becoming.

So, I thank Nat and the retreat for giving me the space to dissolve. I thank the people who witnessed me without needing me to perform. I thank the butterfly for showing up over and over, gently whispering that change is possible, even in the dark.
And I thank the part of me that said yes to this trip. Even when I didn't feel ready. Even when I didn't have a plan.

Beyond metamorphosis lies a kind of beauty I never expected: a life I didn't have to earn, only embrace.

To anyone walking through the dark, unsure of who they are or what they want, I offer this: let yourself melt. Let the old identity dissolve. Let go of who you think you should be.

The wings will come.

You are not breaking. You are becoming.

NB: Julie Fisher, of the Ultimate 48 Hour publishing team, invited me to join this retreat. I had just published my first book, in which I had spent almost nine months working with the publishing team (Julie and Vivi) to move through the finalisation of my book and the publishing process.

I said 'Yes' to the trip, because I wanted to meet Nat and her team in person. I felt so close to Julie and Vivi. They had helped and supported me so much through the transformative process of publishing my book.

Before the trip, a lot of fear and resistance came up. I was in poor health and I was feeling like I shouldn't spend the money on myself. However, I am really glad I pushed through it all and joined this trip. I needed it. The time spent with Nat, Julie, Vivi, Wendy, and the other authors was precious and life-changing.

✧ Actionable Insights: Dissolving Through the Chrysalis ✧

1. **Honour Your Energy Cycles**
   Learn to recognise the rhythms of your body and mind. Instead of forcing productivity during low-energy periods, give yourself permission to rest. Your worth isn't tied to your output.

2. **Trust the Power of Dissolution**
   Transformation often requires letting go of who you thought you were. If you're feeling lost or identity-less, you're not failing – you're in the chrysalis. Trust that the new form will emerge in time.

3. **Name Your Truths, Even the Uncomfortable Ones**
   Whether it's admitting to depression or realising you don't love something you thought you should, self-awareness is the starting point for real change. Say it out loud. Let it land.

4. **Create to Heal**
   Creativity isn't a luxury – it's a lifeline. Draw, write, move, sing. Let your creative practice be the bridge between who you are now and who you're becoming.

5. **Say Yes Before You're Ready**
   If something nudges your spirit – an opportunity, a connection, a trip – trust it. Sometimes the breakthrough you're seeking won't come until you show up and surrender to what unfolds.

A gorgeous sunrise to wake up to every day.

Sydney and Nat at the White Night.

Hosting a moon ritual for the retreat group.

Sydney hosting the moon ceremony on the beach.

About Sydney Francis

Reverend Sydney Francis is a facilitator, artist, spiritual leader, and author of *Activating Lunar Alchemy*. Her 30-plus-year study and practice of art, astrology, healing and the sacred mysteries illuminate her alchemical work with the moon cycle and personal transformative practices.

Sydney has an MFA in Interdisciplinary Art from *Goddard College*, a Master's in Theology, and a Master's in Healing Arts from the *Healing Light Center Church*. She is an ordained minister, as well as a certified wholeness coach and emotional trauma healer.

Find out more at www.soulgardener.me

CHAPTER 10 - ALICIA BUXTON

LEARN AND GAIN FROM LIKE-MINDED PEOPLE

"Try and try until you succeed."
Alicia Buxton

I arrived at the ferry terminal trying to remember Jules's instructions given to us on our *Zoom* meeting. Whether to turn left or right, but to my surprise, as I got in the sliding door, everybody was there waiting. Natasa's organising and time schedules from the start to finish were amazing. She even took a headcount to make sure that everybody was there.

I was quickly introduced to everyone and felt welcome. I felt comfortable straightaway with the group. Everyone bonded with everyone as if we had known each one before.

Luba and I bonded straightaway because of our seasickness issue. I gave her a motion sickness band that you put on your wrist to avoid seasickness. And she gave me a can of *Sprite* to take just in case. How sweet of her.

I straightaway felt the care and compassion not only of Luba, but everyone. How everybody helped each other fill the forms for transfers. For me, the start of this collaborative retreat was positive and I felt happy just meeting the group for the first time.

I felt well accepted by the group considering my age and mobility issues. I would honestly say everybody looked after me, helping me climbing up and down steps. I just love them all. Especially going to the second floor of the resort where they did not have elevator access going to my room. I was moved to the first floor, thanks to Natasa's caring nature.

Being with like-minded people is incredible. Since we are authors, we've all had the experience of the ups and downs of life. At the same time, we are clearly aware on how to express it mentally and verbally, besides from just writing our God-given talents.

What truly impressed me with each and every person was how they wholeheartedly listened to you. That to me is a big plus. They give you their time and communicated their opinions and were not in a hurry. I found it amazing that they made time for me.

I've lived in Sydney for 49 years and this was the first time I'd encountered a group of people like this. On reflection, I loved the attention that I got. Not generalising, maybe people in Sydney are too busy and time poor. Or maybe everybody, including me, had lots of time to listen because we were on holiday mode. Maybe, but I loved the feeling of relaxed communication.

LEARN AND GAIN FROM LIKE-MINDED PEOPLE

I also loved how everyone communicated it in our group messenger. Everybody shared the piece of the action they were doing. Some were snorkelling or doing aerial yoga, others playing golf or just relaxing at the beach.

At this retreat, there was never a dull moment. We were always on the go but not stressed out. Nat was our group leader and she had planned everything from beginning to the end. Her planning and leadership and organising the whole team/group was flawless. There was also care and respect to all with her leadership. Like the throwing of the beach ball experience, meaning your chance to speak up once you got the ball. What an excellent idea.

I think what opened the door to each other's hearts and minds was the first day of our workshop, a self-introduction, our names and where we are from and something about ourselves and our books.

This really helped us to understand each other better. Each one of us had a story to tell. Very interesting. We were all from different countries like the USA, Canada, one from UK, some Queensland, Melbourne and two from Sydney and Mosman. 17 authors from different upbringing, culture and books.

Not only that, but you could also ask each author about their books and why they wrote it. What their main objectives on writing their books were. Like interviewing an author live. Talking to authors face to face. How good is that?

I liked the venue – *Club Med* on Bintan Island. I want to call it 'limitless or unlimited' since our deal was all inclusive – I loved the unlimited drinks, cocktails and the choice of meals were either buffet or a la carte.

The games and activities continued throughout the days. Fantastic shows and entertainment happened every night. All we had to do was join in and enjoy ourselves. We were never short of people around helping us. Incredible, I loved it.

The moment of adventure for me was when Luba, Carmen and myself went to the tour of Bintan Island. It was six hours of learning about the island. We were shown the handy craft centre, the Buddha's temple, the blue lake and the sand. Then we had a smorgasbord seafood lunch in the middle of the lake. It was amazing; what an experience. The best part of that experience was that we did not know how it would unfold, no agenda, just going with the flow. How exciting.

The Blue Lake on the tour around Bintan Island.

I have learned so much from each one of these wonderful, talented, and caring authors. Each one had special knowledgeable answers to questions during our workshops.

Here are the best business tips I picked up:

- The harder I work, the luckier I get.
- Never ever cancel or delay an event.
- The more fun you have, the more money you make.
- Follow your dreams.

I also loved the tips from Natasa for success in business like:

- Love sales <u>and</u> marketing.
- Always upsell in sales.
- It's a numbers game!
- Always consider sales with the highest conversion rate.
- Where there are people, there are opportunities.
- Follow up, follow up, follow up.

One word of wisdom from me to share to everyone reading this chapter is, 'What is holding you back?' What I mean is… When you reach a point that you stop or get stuck or do not have the motivation or energy to continue whatever you are doing, ask yourself, 'Why?' What is holding you back?

If your answer is, 'I am fearful', or 'I'm tired' or 'I have no guts', whatever it is, try to analyse your answer as to why why and make a decision. The answer will give you the solution and resilience, motivation and energy to do something about the why and then justify the why and continue.

This is good words of wisdom to use if you get stuck in writing your book.

What is stopping you?

This author's retreat is a transformative experience that is worth considering if you are open to change in your life, it you love fun and if you like learning from likeminded people. I do not have any hesitation recommending this retreat to anyone. I am booked to join next year's retreat in Bali.

Come and join us and I promise you will love it.

Meeting at 5am to watch the sunrise in Bintan.

LEARN AND GAIN FROM LIKE-MINDED PEOPLE

Learning and having fun in the training room.

Loving Bintan and the whole experience.

About Alicia Buxton

Alicia Buxton is a child care advocate. She has worked as child care Director and Educator for 37 years. Over the years, she has demonstrated her profound love and care for the children, parents and staff. Alicia's book, *The True Miracles of Jesus, i*s about the miracles that happened in her life. She is a member of *Toastmasters International*, a non-profit organisation for improving your public speaking and personal growth since 2009.

In addition, Alicia was awarded Canterbury Business Person of the Year in 2013 for her business commitment, integrity and leadership. In 2015, Alicia founded *Divine Mercy Toastmasters Club* in Camperdown NSW.

Alicia is also an advocate of Evangelisation towards Go Make Disciples and the St. Joseph Catholic Church Camperdown Catechist and RCIA coordinator, which is about children and adults wanting to become a Catholic, Baptised, Confirmed and learn about Jesus and the scriptures. Alicia's goal of writing her book is to make known to others the love of Jesus.

Alicia is available and willing to speak about her miracle experiences to support groups, religious organisation and schools.

To engage Alicia to speak at your venue or events, you can contact her via email at *abuxton333@gmail.com*

CHAPTER 11 - ZOE MACBEAN

JUST START, THEN KEEP MOVING. YOUR PATH WILL APPEAR.

*"First say to yourself what you would be;
and then do what you have to do."*
(Epictetus)

Somewhere around age 50, I very suddenly lost my tolerance for bullshit – especially my own. A friend had made an offhand comment about having 'more yesterdays than tomorrows' and I realised some major life evaluation was in order.

My days were spent racing from one task to another, ticking off items on my to-do list yet somehow never getting to the things that really mattered to me. I was hardly doing anything I actually enjoyed – I was just being busy. All day. Every day.

Decluttering isn't just for homes. It's also for bodies and schedules, relationships and behaviours, dreams and goals. So, I set to work. Old and beloved pair of jeans that didn't fit any more? Gone. Extra kitchen gadgets? Gone. Side hustles that brought in a few bucks but ate up my time? Gone. Limiting beliefs that kept me stuck? Gone. Marriage that I'd worked so hard to save but was clearly dead in the water? Also gone.

The process was painful and took longer than it should but, when it was done, what was left was...

Me.

Someone I almost didn't recognise or remember.

And, hidden away in my heart, my lifelong dreams, my wish list, my true goals.

One of the things that really should have been tossed was a book outline and a few pages of notes. The date I'd put on it was horrifying – I had spent 12 years *not* writing a book.

Oh, sure, I'd puttered with it now and then. Just enough to know that it was worth writing and that I really had no idea how to complete the project. I made a decision to either finish it or admit defeat and chuck it.

I started reading books on self-publishing and hunting for writing groups but nothing seemed to click until I signed up for a free online workshop with *Ultimate 48 Hour Author*. I had expected an hour of sales talk and maybe one or two tips I could use. My plan was to tidy my office area while the workshop played in the background. Three hours and several pages of notes later, I knew I'd found the help I needed to get my book finished and out into the world.

There was just one tiny problem. The coaching was going to cost thousands. Truly not an expense I could justify. And yet, there was the strongest sense that this was the correct path. I could feel that tell-tale thrum of excitement and resonance that marks all of my best and scariest decisions.

I talked it over with my partner and we both agreed that it was a brilliant program but not in our budget. We'd had an epic windstorm earlier in the year and a huge tree had fallen on the bridge that we used to access our property. We were still able to walk across it, but it wasn't safe to drive on and replacing it was going to cost about half a million dollars more than our insurance would cover.

The situation was pretty dire but somehow, I found myself saying out loud that we were going to find a solution. Meanwhile, I would keep working on my book with the tips I'd learned in the workshop. Come hell or high water, it would be written.

Within days of that decision, the insurance company cut us a cheque that would cover about a fifth of a bridge and wished us luck. Freaking out would have been totally justified but I couldn't shake the feeling that things were going to work out.

So, I wasn't all that surprised when, just days later, our neighbour found us a second-hand bridge and a no-nonsense contractor willing to install it. When the job was done and the crew was paid, there was enough left over to pay for the coaching.

When the Universe sends a gift like that, the message is clear and the correct response is massive, rapid action. I cleared my calendar, booked my hotel and went on my first ever author retreat. I made more progress on my book in 48 hours than in the previous 12 years and, more importantly, acquired the skills and strategies needed to make my book a reality.

Many of the other authors had well-established businesses and were planning to use their books as a 'business card on steroids' and I started to catch a vision of what my book could do for my income. Some authors were on their second or even third books and I remember thinking they wouldn't be doing it again if they hadn't seen results with the first one. I also noticed there was a curious energy in knowing that I wasn't alone – that all over the world, there were other writers working on their books at the same time.

I really enjoyed the process of writing but whenever topics would come up around promotion and websites, QR codes and email marketing campaigns, lead magnets and sales funnels, I felt like a pre-schooler who had accidentally stumbled into a university class.

My coaches reassured me again and again not to worry, not to look too far ahead or allow myself to be distracted by what was going on around me – just write the next line, the next paragraph, the next chapter. One thing at a time. Workhorse blinkers on, and full speed ahead until it was done.

They also warned me to expect obstacles to come up and they weren't wrong. There were unexpected surgeries, injuries, family dramas and a host of other challenges I could never have predicted. I attended a second retreat and even took myself away for a self-directed third one.

Each time I started again, it was so hard to get back into the flow of writing but, as one chapter led to another, it got just a little easier. I'd go on the coaching calls and notice that I was no longer the furthest behind.

Then one night, I accidentally finished my book. That is, I was sitting at the back of a cafe during an open mic night, staring at my latest chapter and suddenly realised that if I split it into two chapters and tweaked it a little, it was done. I was so surprised that I burst out laughing. Thank goodness the music was loud – pretty sure I sounded hysterical. I walked on air all the way home.

Now it was time to take the blinkers off again and see what was next. The list was overwhelming. Once again, my coaches broke it down for me. Blinkers back on, made it through editing. This became an almost comfortable routine: blinkers off, freak out, get reassurance and guidance, blinkers on, do the next thing.

And suddenly it was done. Sent to print, published, launched – the works!

Then the blinkers came off again and I suddenly realised I had no clue what to do next. I had been self-employed as a dog trainer for over four decades and still knew almost nothing about running a business.

I had a handful of lovely clients, but I spent more time driving than training and every month was a roller-coaster race to pay the mortgage and put food on the table while worrying constantly about unexpected bills. I had a decent website but otherwise, my infrastructure was pretty much limited to a box of receipts, a very patient accountant and the occasional post on *Facebook*. Something had to change.

First, I turned to business books. All of them had some useful information but most of them assume that you haven't started yet and have time to get all your systems in place. That you have a backup paycheque and thousands to invest. Or you have a six-figure business with multiple employees and you're just looking to improve your bottom line by a few percentage points. There didn't seem to be anything aimed at completely frazzled solo-preneurs being pulled in a million directions by family and clients.

Clearly, I needed a different approach. I've never hesitated to pay top dollar for top quality coaching. It has always rung true for me that if you want to be paid well for your services, you must also be willing to pay someone else for theirs.

On my path as a dog trainer, when I need to upskill, I might start by reading a book or taking an on-line class. If what I learned worked well and my dogs improved, I might invest a little more with that person – maybe attending a workshop or a week-long intensive. If I'm still impressed, I might go as far as flying halfway around the world to spend time with a mentor. Because constantly challenging myself to improve is part of my identity as a trainer.

As a vintage woman looking to reclaim her fitness after injuries and years of 'deferred maintenance', I needed to re-create an identity as someone who deserved a healthy body. I started with a free workshop and saw good results. So I invested a little more time, a little more money and went from hobbling with a cane to getting ready for my first 5k run in over 30 years. Then came the home gym, and now I'm on-track to break my previous records as a powerlifter.

My journey as an author had begun with a free workshop. All I'd had to invest was my time and I'd received good value. Next, I'd joined them for an online retreat for and saw tremendous results. At the end of the retreat, I signed up for a monthly membership. Financially, it was a stretch but I learned so much. It ended up paying for itself many times over.

In each case, the key factor that accelerated my progress was being surrounded by like-minded people. So, when I was offered the chance to spend a week at an in-person retreat with my fellow authors, many of whom were successful business women, I jumped at the chance. I'm still not quite sure how I managed to manifest the money to pay for it but, as usual, when I'm on the right path, the obstacles just seemed to melt away.

My book had launched in November and I'd decided to take a break until after Christmas. Then, in January, I said goodbye to my best working dog. Two weeks later, my beloved stepmother died. And four days later, on what would have been their anniversary, my dad followed her. I could hardly breathe.

I was so glad to have the retreat to look forward to. To, well, *retreat* to. I so needed a safe place to just sit at this crossroads and figure out what was next. I wanted to be closer to the people who had helped me do the last hard thing. To connect face to face. I knew them only from *Zoom* meetings and phone calls, but they'd believed in me and cheered me on, allowing me space as needed but never letting me get too far off track.

I did have a few concerns. What if I spent all that money to go to the other side of the world and it was all just fluff? A little rah-rah, generic motivational talks, a few beach pictures and some partying masquerading as networking. I needn't have worried.

Halfway through the first group session I became aware of two things. First, that there was a palpable energy in the room – an energy that continued to grow from session to session. And second, this is what had been missing in my life.

I've had mentors around my core skills. Trainers, riders, teachers, speakers, lifting coaches. But I've never had business mentors and I'd never been part of a classic mastermind. A dozen women coming together to create a safe space for sharing and creating is a powerful thing.

It shouldn't have surprised me. Since the dawn of time, women have gathered in groups to accomplish all manner of tasks. From quilting bees to the Suffragettes, at an almost atavistic level, we seem to understand that we are all more alike than different, that there is power in unity and that everyone has something of value to contribute.

I really didn't learn how to have female friends until I was in my late 20s.

My lived experience up until then was that female energy was powerful but came with strings attached – usually in the form of a trap or a surprise price tag. Something that could derail you months or even years down the line.

To say my upbringing was a little unconventional is an understatement. I was pretty much raised in the Social Sciences department of a local college. I knew how to be friends with professors and administrators. People my own age? Not so much. Women? Mysterious and more than a little scary. I've gotten better at it but the most I've ever socialised with or collaborated with at one time would be two or three other women, mostly other trainers.

I remember looking at the synopsis for the retreat and wondering if there were really enough sessions to accomplish anything significant – a worry that seems laughable now. To be actively engaged with 12 other women, all working on creating the next chapter of their lives, was so powerful. Watching each one make a deliberate choice to be open, to be vulnerable, to share their true self, was more than a little humbling.

With each session, the energy grew. It was amazing to watch everyone step more fully into their power as creators and to share that energy with everyone in the room. We were all contributing, we were all receiving. Joining that circle was transformative.

There were critiques but no criticisms. There were reframes and gentle nudges and calls to action and it was amazing. I've never before experienced being in a group of women and working together seriously for days with no sense of clique-iness or hidden agendas. Just an amazing sense of accountability, support and encouragement.

Had I encountered some of those questions or concepts before? Certainly. For instance, I've always known my business 'Why' – that part was easy. Why am I a dog trainer? Because it lights me up and is the only thing I've ever wanted to be and because I want to help people find the dog they've always wanted inside the dog they have now. But no one has ever asked me to define the 'What'. Not what did I want to do with my business but what did I want my dog training business to do for *me*. Talk about a huge a-ha moment!

Turns out, what I want is freedom. The freedom to study, to choose the clients I want to work with, to train my own dog, to garden, to travel, to write at least six more books. That means for the next two years, I need to be seriously intentional about my business. Knowing where I want to be sure makes it easier to reverse engineer my path forward.

There's a saying that 'Grief demands a witness' – that it is nearly impossible to move through the grieving process without at least one other human to sit across from you at least once and just *see you* in your grief. That's certainly been true in my life and I'm beginning to think that the same is true of success. Success really wants to be seen, to be acknowledged – preferably by someone qualified to recognise it.

I could tell you about the value of dawn walks on the beach, of meditations in sacred spaces, of laughter shared with new friends and the sheer luxury of unscheduled time, but for me, the magic was in bonding with big group energy. Of speaking out loud the changes I want to make and knowing that when I return next year, there will be witnesses to what I've achieved and a gentle reckoning for what I haven't.

If you are at a crossroads and need to figure out your next step or if you know what you need to do next but it will require creating a whole new identity, find yourself a good retreat – or let it find you.

Enjoying High Tea at the famous Raffles Hotel with my partner Brian and the retreat crew in Singapore.

JUST START, THEN KEEP MOVING. YOUR PATH WILL APPEAR.

Zoe and Nat at the White Night.

Our training room celebration author pic!

About Zoë MacBean

Zoë MacBean is the author of *Housetraining That Works* and is an eclectic trainer of some 40+ years' experience and has never met a stubborn dog — just a whole bunch that were reliable about the wrong things. She's a bit eccentric and perennially scruffy. Chocolate is her fuel of choice.

When she isn't training dogs, she's either cooking, gardening or having hay picked out of her hair by her very patient husband.

She lives on a small farm on Vancouver Island with a foolish young setter, two lazy, semi-retired pack goats, and a very handsome mule.

https://housetrainingfairy.com

CHAPTER 12 - LISA DWYER

NEVER, NEVER GIVE UP

"Be the change you wish to see in the world."
(Gandhi)

Reclaiming Time for my Goals

As I landed in Singapore, I had a strong feeling that something truly special was about to unfold. A radiant rainbow stretched across the sky, its fiery streaks peeking through whispering clouds that seemed to fade gently into the past. It felt like the sky itself was reminding me: beauty still exists – even after the storm.

The slightly overcast skies and the bustle of Singapore jolted me into the present. Where have I been? It was time to reclaim my focus. To recommit to my goals. To finally finish the book I'd started a year ago with *Ultimate 48 Hour Author*.

I was nervous. I was tired. I was excited – all at once.

Leading up to the trip, I nearly cancelled. My brother had fallen seriously ill with a brain injury and infection. For over two and a half months, I had poured every ounce of energy into supporting my family, navigating deep emotional waters, and managing the inevitable friction among siblings. I was running on empty.

But then... I made it.

As I stepped onto the sandy shores of Bintan, everything shifted. The soft, squeaky sand beneath my feet felt grounding, almost medicinal. I took a deep breath and thought, I'm so glad I made it. I'm so glad I'm here.

When I arrived at my room – the furthest away from everyone – it felt like a sanctuary. It overlooked a peaceful billabong, ringed with blooming lilies and flanked by towering six-metre bamboo. Monkeys danced through the trees in the late afternoon light. It was wild, beautiful, and quiet.

A sacred little pocket of peace. The perfect place to rejuvenate and align with self.

The Power of Saying Yes

Before I said yes to the retreat, life had become a blur of crisis management. My brother's brain injury had shattered our family's sense of normal. For months, I'd been holding everyone else together – navigating medical updates, soothing frayed emotions, and playing peacekeeper between family members who were unravelling under pressure.

I was emotionally drained and physically depleted. Writing – something that once gave me life – had been pushed to the farthest corner of my world. My book, my voice, my goals... all on pause.

On top of that, I'd been juggling training as a life coach with the *International Coaching Institute* in Melbourne. What had once inspired me had also fallen by the wayside. I hadn't touched the course in over three months. Not because I didn't care – but because I simply didn't have the bandwidth to care for myself, let alone study.

So, when the invitation to the retreat came, I felt a spark. A small one, yes – but one I hadn't felt in a long time. I wanted to say 'Yes.' Desperately. But guilt crept in immediately. How could I leave? Was this selfish?

But underneath all that noise was a whisper saying, 'You need this. And not just for rest.'

My intention was to lean in, to rediscover my voice as a writer, a coach, a woman who still had dreams. I wanted to learn new skills. I wanted to be stretched. I wanted to realign with my purpose – not the one dictated by crisis, but the one that called to me from deep within.

Even so, I boarded the plane with hesitation. I felt torn, unsure if I was making the right decision. But the moment I arrived, I realised I wasn't just attending a retreat. I was stepping into a sacred space.

A space to reflect. To grow. And most importantly, to remember who I am when I give myself permission to say yes.

The Silence Breaks

It was a conversation with Alicia that cracked something wide open in me. She shared how she had survived a violent carjacking – a moment where everything could have ended. But it didn't, she called it a miracle. And as she spoke, tears welled in my eyes. Her story didn't just move me – it unlocked me. Tomorrow isn't promised.

Because I, too, had survived things that should've broken me. I had stayed silent for 23 years about the abuse I endured – domestic violence that seeped into every part of my life: emotional, physical, financial. I had buried it under resilience, under responsibility, under being 'fine'. But Alicia's story reminded me that survival is not something to hide – it's something to speak.

Later, I sat with Felicity, another powerful woman in the process of writing her own book – hers about women's empowerment after domestic violence. She had recently left her own abusive relationship, and we both knew the harsh truth: just because you leave a perpetrator, doesn't mean they let you go. Especially when children are involved.

Our stories mirrored each other in haunting ways. My children are grown now. They've seen, they know. But still – it's hard for people to grasp the full weight of what I lived through. Sometimes, it's hard for me to believe I survived it.

That night, over cocktails and conversation, I found myself with Julie, the publisher from *Ultimate 48 Hour Author*. She turned to me and said, 'Your story matters.'

It wasn't just encouragement – it was a call to action. I could save lives with my story. But only if I stopped hiding it.

The retreat – and these women – reminded me that my silence served no one. My story is not a wound. It's a weapon. And it's time to use it for good.

Bonding Is Power

Being surrounded by these women – each one a caregiver, a nurturer, a warrior in her own way – was like being wrapped in warmth I didn't realise I'd been missing. We often give so much of ourselves to others that we forget to fill our own cups. But here, on this sacred island, these women helped me remember who I am. And that I deserve to shine, too.

There was something unspoken yet undeniable in the air between us. A mutual recognition. A knowing. We'd all carried heavy things – grief, guilt, trauma, ambition, hope – and yet we laughed, we danced, we shared from the deepest parts of ourselves without fear of judgment. There was no performance, no pretending. Just truth. And love.

The most beautiful part? Knowing these connections won't fade when the retreat ends.

We're already making plans to reunite at next year's retreat. Because once a real connection is made – one that comes from speaking heart-to-heart – it lives on. That's the power of bonding.

I recommend this experience to anyone ready to reconnect with themselves, to find their voice, and to write their best-selling book. Because every story matters. Every voice has a place. And when we speak from the heart with real, raw, authentic honesty – we don't just share a story.

We change lives.

Social media gives us filters and noise. But this? This was eye-to-eye, soul-to-soul, truth in its purest form. It reminded me that we all need to care for each other so much more than we do.

Bonding is not a luxury. It's a lifeline. And when women come together with intention, vulnerability, and courage, it doesn't just light us up – it changes the world.

Permission to Play

There were so many unforgettable moments at the retreat, but one night will stay with me forever – pyjama night.

Our fun pyjama party night.

Yes, you read that right. A group of grown women, in matching and mismatching PJs, slippers, and bathrobes, strolling proudly into dinner like it was a red-carpet event. I'll admit, at first, I felt a little silly. Who goes out dressed for bed? But that was the magic of it. We all did. And we owned it.

That night, the resort just so happened to be hosting karaoke. Of course, we joined. Laughter echoed through the room as we belted out classic ballads, danced around like teenagers, and snapped photos of ourselves in full pyjama glory. No masks. No makeup. Just women being fully, gloriously themselves. We looked ridiculous – and we looked fabulous.

There's something deeply freeing about letting go of appearances and expectations. When you give yourself permission to be playful, to be real, it opens up something sacred. And on that night, joy wasn't just present – it was contagious.

Another moment of bliss? The traditional Indonesian massage followed by a deluxe facial. I nearly melted into the massage table. Surrounded by palm trees, soft music, and the scent of essential oils, I felt every knot of stress unwind. It was heavenly. A sacred pause. The kind of rest that whispers, you are safe to dream again.

The gorgeous setting for our massage experiences.

I'd planned to try archery and the trapeze – but the weather had other ideas. And honestly? Watching others laugh and cheer and fly through the air was enough for me. Sometimes joy isn't in the doing – it's in the sharing.

This retreat reminded me: fun matters. Laughter heals.

And giving yourself the gift of play can refill your spirit faster than any to-do list ever will.

Never, Never Give Up

When I arrived at the *Bond and Beyond Retreat* in Bintan, I was physically, emotionally, and spiritually exhausted. Life had been heavy. I had been stretched so thin caring for others that I'd forgotten how to care for myself. My goals felt distant. My inspiration – gone. I came in tired and unsure, still carrying the weight of fear, doubt, and the quiet ache of wondering if I had lost myself along the way.

But what unfolded over those eight days changed everything.

I left replenished, realigned, and reignited – with clarity, confidence, and a powerful sense of purpose. My book is no longer a 'someday'. It's a now. Not because I need to prove anything – but because the story needs to be told.

It's time to finish *Shut Your Mouth: Why Narcissistic Abuse Is Still Our Silent Killer* and use it to break the silence, empower other women and save lives.

There is something sacred about a space where masks come off, where raw honesty is welcomed, where every story is met with compassion. That's what this retreat offered. And in that space, I remembered who I was.

And I fell in love with the woman I'm becoming.

To anyone on the fence about whether to say yes to an experience like this – say yes. Say yes to yourself. Say yes to your story. Say yes to the healing, the laughter, the truth, the sisterhood, and the structure to move forward.

Because you can stay and die. You can leave and still die. But you can also leave and live. And live well.

In joy.

In peace.

In your power.

We are never too far gone to begin again.

And if there's one thing I want you to remember, it's this:

Never, never give up.

The group being silly with our rabbit ears on Easter Sunday at Bintan.

Lisa modelling the retreat T-shirt.

Chilling with my retreat buddies in Bintan.

Sambuka shots in our PJs - Nat, Lisa, Claire, Vivi, Julie.

About Lisa Dwyer

Lisa Dwyer is a passionate author, life coach, and advocate for truth, healing, and empowerment. Her life's mission is to help women reclaim their voice, rebuild their self-worth, and rise from the silence of trauma and abuse into lives of purpose, power, and peace.

With a background in sugarcane industry, personal training, Autopro franchisee, carer and mentoring as a student at the *International Coaching Institute in Melbourne*, Lisa weaves personal transformation with professional insight. Her forthcoming book, *Shut Your Mouth: Why Narcissistic Abuse Is Still Our Silent Killer*, is a bold and necessary contribution to the conversation around domestic violence and emotional survival.

Lisa's work is rooted in lived experience, emotional honesty, and the unshakable belief that healing is possible – and that every woman's story has the power to change lives. She is committed to helping others not just survive, but thrive, by creating spaces for connection, courage, and clarity.

Whether through her writing, coaching, speaking, or future podcast, Lisa's voice is a guiding light for anyone ready to break cycles, set boundaries, and build the life they deserve.

She lives by this truth: 'You are never too far gone to begin again. And your story matters.'

AFTERWORD

Reflections from the Other Side of Retreat

As I sit and write this afterword, I can't help but smile, because everything I anticipated in the introduction has come to life… and then some.

The stories you've just read are living proof of the magic that happens when we step out of our daily routines and give ourselves permission to *pause*. Just as I knew it would, the Bond & Beyond Retreat sparked transformation, not through rigid schedules or forced outcomes, but through space, spontaneity, connection, and presence.

Each person who attended brought their own energy, experiences, and openness to whatever might unfold - and unfold it did. The insights, ideas, and inner shifts shared in this book weren't planned. They emerged naturally, as they always do, when we stop pushing and start listening.

What I love most about this journey, and what I hope came through in every chapter, is the reminder that **doing less really does help**

us become more. More aligned. More energised. More ourselves. And in that space, real creativity and innovation can finally breathe.

So, what now? My hope is that this book has stirred something in you. Maybe a longing to take a break. Maybe a reminder that you're allowed to reset. Maybe even a desire to join us on a future retreat and experience it for yourself.

Whatever it is, honour it. Don't file it away for later. Life isn't meant to be lived in waiting rooms and to-do lists. Make the time, take the leap, and give yourself the space to discover what's waiting for you on the other side of rest.

Thank you for reading. Thank you to all our incredible authors for sharing so openly. And thank you to the version of you that's brave enough to choose a new way forward.

Here's to more memories, more magic, and more moments that matter.

ACKNOWLEDGEMENTS

I would like to thank the gorgeous authors who made this book possible. Thank you for sharing your stories, a-ha moments, and for bringing so much heart (and fun!) to this collaboration. Your vulnerability and wisdom are what breathe life into these pages.

To my author family who continue to be my inspiration and my motivation, you are the reason I step up every day as a coach, business mentor, and entrepreneur. Thank you for trusting me with your stories, for allowing me to walk alongside you, and for reminding me of the power of growth. As I watch you all thrive, I become a better version of myself.

Thank you to my husband Stuart, for holding the fort with our children back home, and the Team in Vivi, Julie and Wendy, who supported me during this retreat and pulled together the beautiful publication that it is. Also, thanks to Lendy and Rai for taking care of business with our other clients back home.

Lastly, to my mum, your famous sayings, 'Who gave you birth?' and 'Every beginning is hard' have become our family's compass. Your strength and humour have been a rock for me.

Thank you for shaping the woman I am today.

Love, Nat

If you are one of our authors, we would love to have you at next year's retreat!

If you are not, join our community first to gain access to this life-changing experience!

JOIN US NEXT YEAR IN BALI!

ULTIMATE RETREAT EFFECT

ULTIMATE RETREAT EFFECT

MERUSAKA GALLERY

Join us for an extraordinary week where authors bond, businesses blossom, and book marketing ideas are shared. After the resounding success of our 2024 retreat in Phuket and 2025 retreat in Bintan (check out our Videos and photos here https://bit.ly/phuketreel2024), our next destination is in the idyllic paradise of Merusaka Nusa Dua in Bali.

Forge lifelong connections with fellow authors who share your passion and understand your journey. Exchange stories, insights, and laughter, creating bonds that extend beyond the written word. With the tranquil sea whispering secrets of success, map out your next bestseller and business strategy. This retreat isn't just about writing; it's about envisioning and executing a lifestyle that harmonises with your aspirations.

All-Inclusive, All-Inspiring:

From luxurious accommodations to gourmet dining, every aspect of your stay is included. Indulge in Merusaka's hospitality and amenities, freeing your mind to focus on your craft and goals.

What's Included?

- ✓ 7 nights of luxury accommodation at Merusaka Nusa Dua
- ✓ All meals, snacks, and drinks (including spirits and popular cocktails)
- ✓ Branded Retreat Merchandise to remember your experience
- ✓ 3 Exclusive workshops with workbook and sessions with Natasa
    - **Your Ultimate Lifestyle Beyond Bali**
    - **Your Ultimate Business Beyond Bali**
    - **Your Ultimate Book Beyond Bali**
- ✓ One-on-one mentoring to refine your vision and voice when you least expect
- ✓ Opportunities for relaxation and recreation in paradise
- ✓ Networking events to connect and collaborate
- ✓ Fun themed nights to encourage conversation
- ✓ Optional tours and affordable massages just outside the resort

ULTIMATE RETREAT EFFECT

Time	Single Room	Shared Room	Payment Options
By 26 April 2025 Super Early Bird	$4000 AUD	$3000 AUD	$500 deposit PP $500 per month
By 30 June 2025 Early Bird	$4300 AUD	$3330 AUD	$500 deposit PP $500 per month
By 31 Dec. 2025 2025 Price	$4500 AUD	$3500 AUD	$500 PP $1000 per month
By 20 April 2026 2026 Price	$5000 AUD	$4000 AUD	Payment in Full
ALL INCLUSIVE	RESPONSIBLE FOR OWN FLIGHTS	Non - Refundable DEPOSIT	Chip away with Payment Plan
Pay in full now SAVE $100 off Total			

Not included:

You will need to get your own return flights to Denpasar Bali.

Cancellation and Refund Terms:

$500 Non – Refundable deposit and full payment is non-refundable under 90 days from travel. Please ensure you get Travel Insurance in case of unexpected circumstances.

All prices in Australian Dollars

Note on pricing: These prices are adjusted from the resort quote to accommodate for project management, customer service, conference room hire, merchandise creation and workshops attendance.

ACKNOWLEDGEMENTS

ULTIMATE RETREAT EFFECT

APPLICATION FORM

PART A - PERSONAL DETAILS

Title: _____ First Name: _____ Last Name _____

Preferred name (if different): _____

Mobile: _____ Email address: _____

Passport No: _____ Expiry Date: _____

Postal Address:

Address: _____ City: _____

State: _____ Postcode: _____ Country: _____

PART B – PAYMENT DETAILS

☐ **CREDIT CARD:** Please note a 1.7% surcharge applies

  NAME: _____

  NUMBER: _____ EXPIRY: ___ / ___ CCV _____

  AMOUNT: $ _____

  Signature: _____

☐ Direct Deposit (Australia Only) - Ultimate 48 Hour Author BSB 013 333 A/C 9040 19345
  (If payment plan taken up Ezypay will be set up after the Deposit for the monthly instalments)
  Room selected: _____

  Total price being paid: $ _____

  Sharing room with: _____

APPENDIX A

NAT'S PACKING CHECKLIST FOR TROPICAL DESTINATIONS

Clothes

- ○ Travel in runners and _____
- ○ 3 vests
- ○ 3 dresses
- ○ 2 shorts
- ○ 1 skirt
- ○ Exercise bra
- ○ Strapless bra and stick-on nipple covers
- ○ 3 undies (wash and wear)
- ○ 7 bikinis (LOL) or more depends on # of days
- ○ 2 thongs (Black & white)
- ○ Fancy dress nights stuff
- ○ 1 cap/visor
- ○ 2 pairs of sunglasses and any accessories you would normally wear (e.g. bangles, earrings, head scarfs etc)

Toiletries (only under 100ml can go in hand luggage):

- Sunscreen body and face
- Cleanser, BB Cream, glow bronzer
- Make up brushes, tweezers, small scissors and nail file (<u>DO NOT put in hand luggage</u>)
- Body cream
- Period supplies, if needed
- Hair brush, wigs, ties, pins, product for hair if needed
- Toothbrush, toothpaste and dental floss
- Deodorant, tissues for hand luggage
- Panadol, anti-histamine, Imodium, mosquito repellent and any other medications/supplements

Electronics:

- Laptop and charger (in hand luggage with you)
- Phone and iPad and charger (in hand luggage with you)
- Destination country plug converter
- Plugs with USB ports
- Portable speaker with charger if you want

Stationary and other (all in hand luggage):

- Wallet only with necessary license and credit cards and cash if needed (depends on country)
- Passport – has it got six months before it expires on your last day of travel?
- Travel insurance – have you organised it?

NAT'S PACKING CHECKLIST FOR TROPICAL DESTINATIONS

- ○ Visas – do you need one for that country?
- ○ 3 pens and 2 highlighters
- ○ Notebook and diary
- ○ Physical books you like to read
- ○ Any other activities you may like to do (colouring in, crossword books, magazines)
- ○ Remember to download movies or shows on your device for your flight and any books you may like to read on your device before you leave.

NB: Pack in large suitcase for check in (leave room for shopping to bring home). Travel on board with a backpack (much easier to carry on and off and can fit under seat to access all you need). Choose backpacks with lots of pockets (Samsonite has great ones) categorise when you pack. Carry laptop in backpack and use soft case cover to protect it.

APPENDIX B

Please find below and in the upcoming pages the *Bond and Beyond* workbook created for our conference sessions, to dig deeper into our values and what our intentions were *Beyond Bintan* – lifestyle, business and book.

PRE WORK AHEAD OF THE RETREAT...

Values Elicitation Exercise – Dr. John Demartini's Process

Instructions: The answers to the questions below should come easily to you. Don't overthink them, just list and go to the next question. It is ok if some answers repeat in multiple areas.

This exercise will help us to work through the retreat sessions with more accuracy and better outcome for you.

Let's go....

1. How do you fill your personal or professional space? Identify the three items that occupy your space the most.

1. _____
2. _____
3. _____

2. How do you spend your time? Determine the three activities you dedicate most of your time to when awake.

1. _____
2. _____
3. _____

3. How do you spend your energy? List the three activities that energize you the most.

1. _____
2. _____
3. _____

4. How do you spend your money? Identify the top three areas where you consistently allocate your financial resources.

1. _____
2. _____
3. _____

5. Where are you most organized? Highlight the three areas in your life where you maintain the highest level of order and organization.

1. _____
2. _____
3. _____

6. Where are you most reliable, disciplined, and focused? Specify the three activities or responsibilities where you exhibit the most reliability and discipline.

1. _____
2. _____
3. _____

7. What do you think about? Note the three topics or goals you consistently contemplate and that are materializing in your life.

1. _____
2. _____
3. _____

8. What do you visualize? Describe the three visions or mental images you frequently envision about your future that are becoming reality.

1. _____
2. _____
3. _____

9. What do you internally dialogue about? Identify the three topics you engage in self-talk about most frequently.

1. _____
2. _____
3. _____

10. What do you talk about in social settings? List the three subjects you most often bring up in conversations with others.

1. _____
2. _____
3. _____

11. What inspires you? Determine the three individuals or things that inspire you the most.

1. _____
2. _____
3. _____

12. What goals stand out in your life and have stood the test of time? Identify the three long-term goals you are actively pursuing.

1. _____
2. _____
3. _____

13. What do you love to learn and read about most? Specify the top three topics you are most passionate about studying or reading.

1. _____
2. _____
3. _____

Now, look at your answers and find the five most common ones that have come up and list them below:

1. _____
2. _____
3. _____
4. _____
5. _____

Bring these to the retreat!

BEYOND LIFESTYLE
Vision Mapping Exercise

Describe your ideal average day from morning to night. Where are you? Who are you with? What are you doing?

APPENDIX B

BEYOND LIFESTYLE
Freedom Test

Where in your life do you currently feel free?

_____
_____
_____
_____
_____
_____
_____

Where do you feel stuck?

_____
_____
_____
_____
_____
_____
_____

What would need to change for you to feel more in control?

_____
_____
_____
_____
_____
_____
_____

CORE VALUES DEEP DIVE — THE KEY TO GETTING WHAT YOU WANT!

List your top 5 core values. Are you living in alignment with them? If not, what needs to change?

_____
_____
_____
_____
_____
_____
_____

List the top 5 values that came out of the Pre-Work exercise?

_____
_____
_____
_____
_____
_____
_____

How are these different?

_____
_____
_____
_____
_____

APPENDIX B

DESIGNING YOUR IDEAL YEAR

What are 3 major changes you will implement in the next 12 months to move toward your ideal lifestyle?

BEYOND BUSINESS

Why are you in business?

TO _____
(Contribution)

SO THAT _____
(Impact)

Examples:

EXAMPLE BUSINESS WHY:

TO PUBLISH AND MONETISE A BOOK SO THAT PEOPLE CAN CREATE SUCCESS ON A PERSONAL AND GLOBAL SCALE.

EXAMPLE PERSONAL WHY'S

JULIE:

To inspire and educate people so that the world sees the beauty in disability.

VIVI:

To give others the voice so that people feel included and supported.

WENDY:

To empower people to grow so that they can achieve their highest values in life.

NAT:

To give women courage so that they become independent self-made millionaires.

STU:

To create a supportive and attentive environment so that others shine brightly.

APPENDIX B

MAP OUT YOUR SALES FUNNEL FOR YOUR BUSINESS BELOW
(If you don't have one, let's create one now)

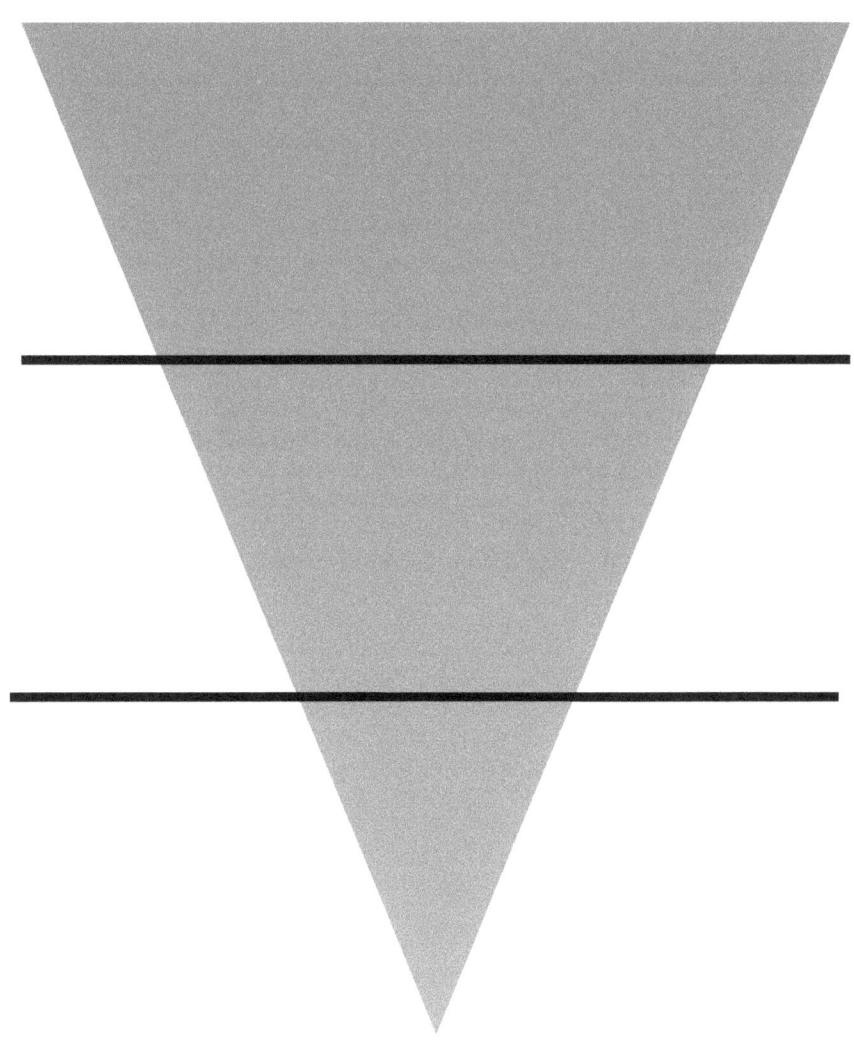

YOUR DREAM BUSINESS

What does your ideal business look like in 12 months? How much revenue? How many clients? How much time do you spend working?

_____
_____
_____
_____
_____
_____
_____
_____
_____
_____
_____
_____

What do you need to STOP doing and START doing?

STOP: _____
_____
_____
_____
_____

START: _____
_____
_____
_____
_____

APPENDIX B

SCALING & SYSTEMS

What infrastructure needs to be there to achieve your goals?

_____
_____
_____
_____
_____
_____
_____
_____
_____
_____

What do you need to STOP doing and START doing?

1. Networking: I will attend _____ a week _____ a month and _____ in a year.

2. Social Media: I will post _____ a week and stay consistent on _____ and _____ social media platforms.

3. Collaborations: I will build and nurture _____ relationships in the next 12 months.

4. Email Marketing: I will send _____ emails per week.

5. Speaking: I will find and lock in _____ speaking opportunities.

6. Online seminars/speaking: I will find _____ opportunities.

7. Live Events: I will host _____ live events.

8. Lead Magnet: I will create _____ lead magnets.

9. Infrastructure: I will create _____, _____ and _____ for my business.

10. Videos: I will record _____ videos in the next 12 months.

BEYOND BOOK

Author's Mindset Shift

What do you want your book to achieve for you? List at least three outcomes (e.g., credibility, business growth, speaking engagements).

_____
_____
_____
_____
_____
_____

Leveraging Your Book

List 3-5 ways you can use your book to open doors for new opportunities.

_____
_____
_____
_____
_____
_____

30/60/90-Day Book Plan

Outline three key marketing or promotional activities you will commit to over the next 90 days.

_____
_____
_____
_____
_____
_____

APPENDIX B

BONUS EXERCISES

YOUR VISION BOARD

Write out a list of images below for your Vision Board, then look them up online and save them somewhere so that when you get home you can print and stick them on a board to hang somewhere you will see on a regular basis.

Ideas on what to look for:

- Ideal body/health
- Family (perhaps a photo of your happy family)
- Dream car
- Dream home
- Dream business/career
- Travel goals
- Ideal income
- Property/Investment goals
- Contribution goals

ULTIMATE 12 MONTH GOALS

It's the 31ˢᵗ of December _____ and I…

      Reward:	**Achieved** **YES / NO** **SUCCESS** **PERCENTAGE** _____ %
      Reward:	**Achieved** **YES / NO** **SUCCESS** **PERCENTAGE** _____ %
      Reward:	**Achieved** **YES / NO** **SUCCESS** **PERCENTAGE** _____ %
      Reward:	**Achieved** **YES / NO** **SUCCESS** **PERCENTAGE** _____ %
      Reward:	**Achieved** **YES / NO** **SUCCESS** **PERCENTAGE** _____ %

APPENDIX B

ULTIMATE 2ⁿᵈ QUARTER GOALS

It's the 30ᵗʰ of June _____ and I...

_____ _____ _____ _____ _____ _____ _____ Reward:	**Achieved** **YES / NO** **SUCCESS** **PERCENTAGE** _____%
_____ _____ _____ _____ _____ _____ _____ Reward:	**Achieved** **YES / NO** **SUCCESS** **PERCENTAGE** _____%
_____ _____ _____ _____ _____ _____ _____ Reward:	**Achieved** **YES / NO** **SUCCESS** **PERCENTAGE** _____%
_____ _____ _____ _____ _____ _____ _____ Reward:	**Achieved** **YES / NO** **SUCCESS** **PERCENTAGE** _____%
_____ _____ _____ _____ _____ _____ _____ Reward:	**Achieved** **YES / NO** **SUCCESS** **PERCENTAGE** _____%

YOUR BUCKET LIST

1. _____
2. _____
3. _____
4. _____
5. _____
6. _____
7. _____
8. _____
9. _____
10. _____
11. _____
12. _____
13. _____
14. _____
15. _____
16. _____
17. _____
18. _____
19. _____
20. _____
21. _____
22. _____
23. _____
24. _____
25. _____

APPENDIX B

YOUR BUCKET LIST

26. _____
27. _____
28. _____
29. _____
30. _____
31. _____
32. _____
33. _____
34. _____
35. _____
36. _____
37. _____
38. _____
39. _____
40. _____
41. _____
42. _____
43. _____
44. _____
45. _____
46. _____
47. _____
48. _____
49. _____
50. _____

YOUR BUCKET LIST

51. _____
52. _____
53. _____
54. _____
55. _____
56. _____
57. _____
58. _____
59. _____
60. _____
61. _____
62. _____
63. _____
64. _____
65. _____
66. _____
67. _____
68. _____
69. _____
70. _____
71. _____
72. _____
73. _____
74. _____
75. _____

APPENDIX B

YOUR BUCKET LIST

76. _____
77. _____
78. _____
79. _____
80. _____
81. _____
82. _____
83. _____
84. _____
85. _____
86. _____
87. _____
88. _____
89. _____
90. _____
91. _____
92. _____
93. _____
94. _____
95. _____
96. _____
97. _____
98. _____
99. _____
100. _____

NOTES

APPENDIX B

NOTES

NOTES

NOTES

NOTES

NOTES

NOTES

APPENDIX B

NOTES

ULTIMATE RETREAT EFFECT

NOTES

www.ingramcontent.com/pod-product-compliance
Lightning Source LLC
Chambersburg PA
CBHW061217070526
44584CB00029B/3876